Criminal Law/Law

2013

Dr Claire McGourlay, Michael Jefferson and Katie Steiner

LAW120, LAW3007, LAW6028 & LAW6092
The University of Sheffield.

Longman
is an imprint of

Harlow, England • London • New York • Boston • San Francisco • Toronto • Sydney • Singapore • Hong Kong
Tokyo • Seoul • Taipei • New Delhi • Cape Town • Madrid • Mexico City • Amsterdam • Munich • Paris • Milan

Pearson Education Limited
Edinburgh Gate
Harlow
Essex
CM20 2JE
England

and Associated Companies throughout the world

Visit us on the World Wide Web at:
www.pearsoned.co.uk

This Custom Book Edition © 2013 published by Pearson Education Limited

ISBN: 978 1 78236 801 4

Printed and bound in the UK by Clays Ltd, Bungay, Suffolk.

Contents

Alphabetical Contents

Chronological Contents

Acknowledgements

We are grateful to the following for permission to reproduce copyright material:

Council of Europe; The United Nations; UNCITRAL; International Labour Organisation (ILO); World Intellectual Property Organization (WIPO); European Patent Office (EPO); International Union for the Protection of New Varieties of Plants (UPOV); The World Trade Organization (WTO); the Commission for Equality and Human Rights, known as the Equality and Human Rights Commission ('the EHRC'); The World Medical Association (WMA). The Crown Prosecution Service material is reproduced under the terms of the Click-Use licence. OPSI data © Crown copyright and database right.

In some instances we have been unable to trace the owners of copyright material, and we would appreciate any information that would enable us to do so.

Publisher's Preface

This Longman Law Bespoke Statute book has been compiled by your lecturer to contain only those statutory materials relevant to your course and no more.

For the purposes of this statute book, all statutes are treated as fully in force upon receipt of Royal Assent and are printed in the form in which they were law as of June 2012. Any amendments or repeals made by subsequent legislation have been incorporated directly in the relevant text. In particular, insertions or substitutions are indicated by their inclusion in a square bracket and repeals are indicated by an ellipsis within the text. Where an entire section or sub-section has been repealed, this is shown by a full row of dots but the section or sub-section number is retained within the text for reference.

For reasons of space, any supplementary notes or annotations and details of amending legislation have been omitted from this statute book. If required, such details are easily accessible online at http://www.statutelaw.gov.uk/.

Where available, European Union legislation appears in its consolidated version, incorporating amendments made by subsequent legislation silently into the text, but if necessary for reference you can access all European Union legislation in its original form at http://europa.eu/index_en.htm.

Coroners and Justice Act 2009

2009 c. 25

PART 2

CRIMINAL OFFENCES

CHAPTER 1

MURDER, INFANTICIDE AND SUICIDE

PARTIAL DEFENCE TO MURDER: DIMINISHED RESPONSIBILITY

52   **Persons suffering from diminished responsibility (England and Wales)**

(1)   In section 2 of the Homicide Act 1957 (c. 11) (persons suffering from diminished responsibility), for subsection (1) substitute—

"(1)   A person ("D") who kills or is a party to the killing of another is not to be convicted of murder if D was suffering from an abnormality of mental functioning which—

(a)   arose from a recognised medical condition,

(b)   substantially impaired D's ability to do one or more of the things mentioned in subsection (1A), and

(c)   provides an explanation for D's acts and omissions in doing or being a party to the killing.

(1A)   Those things are—

(a)   to understand the nature of D's conduct;

(b)   to form a rational judgment;

(c)   to exercise self-control.

(1B)   For the purposes of subsection (1)(c), an abnormality of mental functioning provides an explanation for D's conduct if it causes, or is a significant contributory factor in causing, D to carry out that conduct."

(2)   In section 6 of the Criminal Procedure (Insanity) Act 1964 (c. 84) (evidence by prosecution of insanity or diminished responsibility), in paragraph (b) for "mind" substitute " mental functioning ".

53   **Persons suffering from diminished responsibility (Northern Ireland)**

(1)   Section 5 of the Criminal Justice Act (Northern Ireland) 1966 (c. 20) (effect, in cases of homicide, of impaired mental responsibility) is amended as follows.

(2)   For subsection (1) substitute—

"(1)   A person ("D") who kills or is a party to the killing of another is not to be convicted of murder if D was suffering from an abnormality of mental functioning which—

(a)   arose from a recognised mental condition,

(b)   substantially impaired D's ability to do one or more of the things mentioned in subsection (1A), and

(c)   provides an explanation for D's acts and omissions in doing or being a party to the killing.

(1A)   Those things are—

(a)   to understand the nature of D's conduct;

(b)   to form a rational judgment;

(c)   to exercise self-control.

(1B)   For the purposes of subsection (1)(c), an abnormality of mental functioning provides an explanation for D's conduct if it causes, or is a significant contributory factor in causing, D to carry out that conduct.

(1C)   Where, but for this section, D would be liable, whether as principal or as accessory, to be convicted of murder, D is liable instead to be convicted of manslaughter."

(3)   In subsection (2), for "subsection (1)" substitute " subsection (1C) ".

(4)   In subsections (4) and (5), for "mental abnormality" substitute " abnormality of mental functioning ".

PARTIAL DEFENCE TO MURDER: LOSS OF CONTROL

54   Partial defence to murder: loss of control

(1)   Where a person ("D") kills or is a party to the killing of another ("V"), D is not to be convicted of murder if—

(a)   D's acts and omissions in doing or being a party to the killing resulted from D's loss of self-control,

(b)   the loss of self-control had a qualifying trigger, and

(c)   a person of D's sex and age, with a normal degree of tolerance and self-restraint and in the circumstances of D, might have reacted in the same or in a similar way to D.

(2)   For the purposes of subsection (1)(a), it does not matter whether or not the loss of control was sudden.

(3)   In subsection (1)(c) the reference to "the circumstances of D" is a reference to all of D's circumstances other than those whose only relevance to D's conduct is that they bear on D's general capacity for tolerance or self-restraint.

(4)   Subsection (1) does not apply if, in doing or being a party to the killing, D acted in a considered desire for revenge.

(5)   On a charge of murder, if sufficient evidence is adduced to raise an issue with respect to the defence under subsection (1), the jury must assume that the defence is satisfied unless the prosecution proves beyond reasonable doubt that it is not.

(6)   For the purposes of subsection (5), sufficient evidence is adduced to raise an issue with respect to the defence if evidence is adduced on which, in the opinion of the trial judge, a jury, properly directed, could reasonably conclude that the defence might apply.

(7)   A person who, but for this section, would be liable to be convicted of murder is liable instead to be convicted of manslaughter.

(8)   The fact that one party to a killing is by virtue of this section not liable to be convicted of murder does not affect the question whether the killing amounted to murder in the case of any other party to it.

55   **Meaning of "qualifying trigger"**

(1)   This section applies for the purposes of section 54.

(2)   A loss of self-control had a qualifying trigger if subsection (3), (4) or (5) applies.

(3)   This subsection applies if D's loss of self-control was attributable to D's fear of serious violence from V against D or another identified person.

(4)   This subsection applies if D's loss of self-control was attributable to a thing or things done or said (or both) which—

    (a)   constituted circumstances of an extremely grave character, and

    (b)   caused D to have a justifiable sense of being seriously wronged.

(5)   This subsection applies if D's loss of self-control was attributable to a combination of the matters mentioned in subsections (3) and (4).

(6)   In determining whether a loss of self-control had a qualifying trigger—

    (a)   D's fear of serious violence is to be disregarded to the extent that it was caused by a thing which D incited to be done or said for the purpose of providing an excuse to use violence;

    (b)   a sense of being seriously wronged by a thing done or said is not justifiable if D incited the thing to be done or said for the purpose of providing an excuse to use violence;

    (c)   the fact that a thing done or said constituted sexual infidelity is to be disregarded.

(7)   In this section references to "D" and "V" are to be construed in accordance with section 54.

56   **Abolition of common law defence of provocation**

(1)   The common law defence of provocation is abolished and replaced by sections 54 and 55.

(2)   Accordingly, the following provisions cease to have effect—

    (a)   section 3 of the Homicide Act 1957 (c. 11) (questions of provocation to be left to the jury);

    (b)   section 7 of the Criminal Justice Act (Northern Ireland) 1966 (c. 20) (questions of provocation to be left to the jury).

Criminal Damage Act 1971

1971 c. 48

1   **Destroying or damaging property.**

(1)   A person who without lawful excuse destroys or damages any property belonging to another intending to destroy or damage any such property or being reckless as to whether any such property would be destroyed or damaged shall be guilty of an offence.

(2)   A person who without lawful excuse destroys or damages any property, whether belonging to himself or another—

(a)   intending to destroy or damage any property or being reckless as to whether any property would be destroyed or damaged; and

(b)   intending by the destruction or damage to endanger the life of another or being reckless as to whether the life of another would be thereby endangered;

shall be guilty of an offence.

(3)   An offence committed under this section by destroying or damaging property by fire shall be charged as arson.

2   **Threats to destroy or damage property.**

A person who without lawful excuse makes to another a threat, intending that that other would fear it would be carried out,—

(a)   to destroy or damage any property belonging to that other or a third person; or

(b)   to destroy or damage his own property in a way which he knows is likely to endanger the life of that other or third person;

shall be guilty of an offence.

3   **Possessing anything with intent to destroy or damage property.**

A person who has anything in his custody or under his control intending without lawful excuse to use it or cause or permit another to use it—

(a)   to destroy or damage any property belonging to some other person; or

(b)   to destroy or damage his own or the user's property in a way which he knows is likely to endanger the life of some other person;

shall be guilty of an offence.

4   **Punishment of offences.**

(1)   A person guilty of arson under section 1 above or of an offence under section 1(2) above (whether arson or not) shall on conviction on indictment be

liable to imprisonment for life.

(2)   A person guilty of any other offence under this Act shall on conviction on indictment be liable to imprisonment for a term not exceeding ten years.

5   "Without lawful excuse."

(1)   This section applies to any offence under section 1(1) above and any offence under section 2 or 3 above other than one involving a threat by the person charged to destroy or damage property in a way which he knows is likely to endanger the life of another or involving an intent by the person charged to use or cause or permit the use of something in his custody or under his control so to destroy or damage property.

(2)   A person charged with an offence to which this section applies, shall, whether or not he would be treated for the purposes of this Act as having a lawful excuse apart from this subsection, be treated for those purposes as having a lawful excuse—

(a)   if at the time of the act or acts alleged to constitute the offence he believed that the person or persons whom he believed to be entitled to consent to the destruction of or damage to the property in question had so consented, or would have so consented to it if he or they had known of the destruction or damage and its circumstances; or

(b)   if he destroyed or damaged or threatened to destroy or damage the property in question or, in the case of a charge of an offence under section 3 above, intended to use or cause or permit the use of something to destroy or damage it, in order to protect property belonging to himself or another or a right or interest in property which was or which he believed to be vested in himself or another, and at the time of the act or acts alleged to constitute the offence he believed—

(i)   that the property, right or interest was in immediate need of protection; and

(ii)   that the means of protection adopted or proposed to be adopted were or would be reasonable having regard to all the circumstances.

(3)   For the purposes of this section it is immaterial whether a belief is justified or not if it is honestly held.

(4)   For the purposes of subsection (2) above a right or interest in property includes any right or privilege in or over land, whether created by grant, licence or otherwise.

(5)   This section shall not be construed as casting doubt on any defence recognised by law as a defence to criminal charges.

6   Search for things intended for use in committing offences of criminal damage.

(1)   If it is made to appear by information on oath before a justice of the peace that there is reasonable cause to believe that any person has in his custody or under his control or on his premises anything which there is reasonable cause to believe has been used or is intended for use without lawful excuse—

(a)   to destroy or damage property belonging to another; or

(b)   to destroy or damage any property in a way likely to endanger the life of another,

the justice may grant a warrant authorising any constable to search for and seize that thing.

(2)   A constable who is authorised under this section to search premises for anything, may enter (if need be by force) and search the premises accordingly and may seize anything which he believes to have been used or to be intended to be used as aforesaid.

(3)   The Police (Property) Act 1897 (disposal of property in the possession of the police) shall apply to property which has come into the possession of the police under this section as it applies to property which has come into the possession of the police in the circumstances mentioned in that Act.

7   Jurisdiction of magistrates' courts.

(1)   . . . .

(2)   No rule of law ousting the jurisdiction of magistrates' courts to try offences where a dispute of title to property is involved shall preclude magistrates' courts from trying offences under this Act, or any other offences of destroying or damaging property.

8   . . . .

9   Evidence in connection with offences under this Act.

A person shall not be excused, by reason that to do so may incriminate that person or the [spouse or civil partner] of that person of an offence under this Act—

(a)   from answering any question put to that person in proceedings for the recovery or administration of any property, for the execution of any trust or for an account of any property or dealings with property; or

(b)   from complying with any order made in any such proceedings;

but no statement or admission made by a person in answering a question put or complying with an order made as aforesaid shall, in proceedings for an offence under this Act, be admissible in evidence against that person or (unless they [married or became civil partners after the making of the statement or admission) against the spouse or civil partner] of that person.

10   Interpretation.

(1)   In this Act "property" means property of a tangible nature, whether real or personal, including money and—

(a)   including wild creatures which have been tamed or are ordinarily kept in captivity, and any other wild creatures or their carcasses if, but only if, they have been reduced into possession which has not been lost or abandoned or are in the course of being reduced into possession; but

(b)   not including mushrooms growing wild on any land or flowers, fruit or foliage of a plant growing wild on any land.

For the purposes of this subsection "mushroom" includes any fungus and "plant" includes any shrub or tree.

(2)   Property shall be treated for the purposes of this Act as belonging to any person—

(a)   having the custody or control of it;

(b)   having in it any proprietary right or interest (not being an equitable interest arising only from an agreement to transfer or grant an interest); or

(c)   having a charge on it.

(3)   Where property is subject to a trust, the persons to whom it belongs shall be so treated as including any person having a right to enforce the trust.

(4)   Property of a corporation sole shall be so treated as belonging to the corporation notwithstanding a vacancy in the corporation.

[(5)   For the purposes of this Act a modification of the contents of a computer shall not be regarded as damaging any computer or computer storage medium unless its effect on that computer or computer storage medium impairs its physical condition.]

Criminal Justice Act 1988

1988 c. 33

PART V
JURISDICTION, IMPRISONMENT, FINES, ETC.

JURISDICTION

39   **Common assault and battery to be summary offences.**

Common assault and battery shall be summary offences and a person guilty of either of them shall be liable to a fine not exceeding level 5 on the standard scale, to imprisonment for a term not exceeding six months, or to both.

Corporate Manslaughter and Corporate Homicide Act 2007

2007 c. 19

CORPORATE MANSLAUGHTER AND CORPORATE HOMICIDE

1   **The offence**

    (1)   An organisation to which this section applies is guilty of an offence if the way in which its activities are managed or organised—

        (a)   causes a person's death, and

        (b)   amounts to a gross breach of a relevant duty of care owed by the organisation to the deceased.

    (2)   The organisations to which this section applies are—

        (a)   a corporation;

        (b)   a department or other body listed in Schedule 1;

        (c)   a police force;

        (d)   a partnership, or a trade union or employers' association, that is an employer.

    (3)   An organisation is guilty of an offence under this section only if the way in which its activities are managed or organised by its senior management is a substantial element in the breach referred to in subsection (1).

    (4)   For the purposes of this Act—

        (a)   "relevant duty of care" has the meaning given by section 2, read with sections 3 to 7;

        (b)   a breach of a duty of care by an organisation is a "gross" breach if the conduct alleged to amount to a breach of that duty falls far below what can reasonably be expected of the organisation in the circumstances;

        (c)   "senior management", in relation to an organisation, means the persons who play significant roles in—

            (i)   the making of decisions about how the whole or a substantial part of its activities are to be managed or organised, or

            (ii)   the actual managing or organising of the whole or a substantial part of those activities.

    (5)   The offence under this section is called—

        (a)   corporate manslaughter, in so far as it is an offence under the law of England and Wales or Northern Ireland;

        (b)   corporate homicide, in so far as it is an offence under the law of Scotland.

(6)   An organisation that is guilty of corporate manslaughter or corporate homicide is liable on conviction on indictment to a fine.

(7)   The offence of corporate homicide is indictable only in the High Court of Justiciary.

RELEVANT DUTY OF CARE

2   **Meaning of "relevant duty of care"**

(1)   A "relevant duty of care", in relation to an organisation, means any of the following duties owed by it under the law of negligence—

(a)   a duty owed to its employees or to other persons working for the organisation or performing services for it;

(b)   a duty owed as occupier of premises;

(c)   a duty owed in connection with—

(i)   the supply by the organisation of goods or services (whether for consideration or not),

(ii)   the carrying on by the organisation of any construction or maintenance operations,

(iii)   the carrying on by the organisation of any other activity on a commercial basis, or

(iv)   the use or keeping by the organisation of any plant, vehicle or other thing;

(d)   a duty owed to a person who, by reason of being a person within subsection (2), is someone for whose safety the organisation is responsible.

(2)   A person is within this subsection if—

(a)   he is detained at a custodial institution or in a custody area at a court [, a police station or customs premises];

[(aa)   he is detained in service custody premises;]

(b)   he is detained at a removal centre or short-term holding facility;

(c)   he is being transported in a vehicle, or being held in any premises, in pursuance of prison escort arrangements or immigration escort arrangements;

(d)   he is living in secure accommodation in which he has been placed;

(e)   he is a detained patient.

(3)   Subsection (1) is subject to sections 3 to 7.

(4)   A reference in subsection (1) to a duty owed under the law of negligence includes a reference to a duty that would be owed under the law of negligence but for any statutory provision under which liability is imposed in place of liability under that law.

(5)   For the purposes of this Act, whether a particular organisation owes a duty of care to a particular individual is a question of law.
The judge must make any findings of fact necessary to decide that question.

(6)   For the purposes of this Act there is to be disregarded—

(a)   any rule of the common law that has the effect of preventing a duty of care from being owed by one person to another by reason of the fact that they are jointly engaged in unlawful conduct;

(b)   any such rule that has the effect of preventing a duty of care from being owed to a person by reason of his acceptance of a risk of harm.

(7)   In this section—

"construction or maintenance operations" means operations of any of the following descriptions—

(a)   construction, installation, alteration, extension, improvement, repair, maintenance, decoration, cleaning, demolition or dismantling of—

(i)   any building or structure,

(ii)   anything else that forms, or is to form, part of the land, or

(iii)   any plant, vehicle or other thing;

(b)   operations that form an integral part of, or are preparatory to, or are for rendering complete, any operations within paragraph (a);

"custodial institution" means a prison, a young offender institution, a secure training centre, a young offenders institution, a young offenders centre, a juvenile justice centre or a remand centre;

["customs premises" means premises wholly or partly occupied by persons designated under section 3 (general customs officials) or 11 (customs revenue officials) of the Borders, Citizenship and Immigration Act 2009;]

"detained patient" means—

(a)   a person who is detained in any premises under—

(i)   Part 2 or 3 of the Mental Health Act 1983 (c. 20) ("the 1983 Act"), or

(ii)   Part 2 or 3 of the Mental Health (Northern Ireland) Order 1986 (S.I. 1986/595 (N.I. 4)) ("the 1986 Order");

(b)   a person who (otherwise than by reason of being detained as mentioned in paragraph (a)) is deemed to be in legal custody by—

(i)   section 137 of the 1983 Act,

(ii)   Article 131 of the 1986 Order, or

(iii)   article 11 of the Mental Health (Care and Treatment) (Scotland) Act 2003 (Consequential Provisions) Order 2005 (S.I. 2005/2078);

(c)   a person who is detained in any premises, or is otherwise in custody, under the Mental Health (Care and Treatment) (Scotland) Act 2003 (asp 13) or Part 6 of the Criminal Procedure (Scotland) Act 1995 (c.

46) or who is detained in a hospital under section 200 of that Act of 1995;

"immigration escort arrangements" means arrangements made under section 156 of the Immigration and Asylum Act 1999 (c. 33);

"the law of negligence" includes—

   (a) in relation to England and Wales, the Occupiers' Liability Act 1957 (c. 31), the Defective Premises Act 1972 (c. 35) and the Occupiers' Liability Act 1984 (c. 3);

   (b) in relation to Scotland, the Occupiers' Liability (Scotland) Act 1960 (c. 30);

   (c) in relation to Northern Ireland, the Occupiers' Liability Act (Northern Ireland) 1957 (c. 25), the Defective Premises (Northern Ireland) Order 1975 (S.I. 1975/1039 (N.I. 9)), the Occupiers' Liability (Northern Ireland) Order 1987 (S.I. 1987/1280 (N.I. 15)) and the Defective Premises (Landlord's Liability) Act (Northern Ireland) 2001 (c. 10);

"prison escort arrangements" means arrangements made under section 80 of the Criminal Justice Act 1991 (c. 53) or under section 102 or 118 of the Criminal Justice and Public Order Act 1994 (c. 33);

"removal centre" and "short-term holding facility" have the meaning given by section 147 of the Immigration and Asylum Act 1999;

"secure accommodation" means accommodation, not consisting of or forming part of a custodial institution, provided for the purpose of restricting the liberty of persons under the age of 18.

["service custody premises" has the meaning given by section 300(7) of the Armed Forces Act 2006.]

3   **Public policy decisions, exclusively public functions and statutory inspections**

   (1) Any duty of care owed by a public authority in respect of a decision as to matters of public policy (including in particular the allocation of public resources or the weighing of competing public interests) is not a "relevant duty of care".

   (2) Any duty of care owed in respect of things done in the exercise of an exclusively public function is not a "relevant duty of care" unless it falls within section 2(1)(a), (b) or (d).

   (3) Any duty of care owed by a public authority in respect of inspections carried out in the exercise of a statutory function is not a "relevant duty of care" unless it falls within section 2(1)(a) or (b).

   (4) In this section—

   "exclusively public function" means a function that falls within the prerogative of the Crown or is, by its nature, exercisable only with authority conferred—

       (a) by the exercise of that prerogative, or

(b) by or under a statutory provision;

"statutory function" means a function conferred by or under a statutory provision.

4   **Military activities**

(1)   Any duty of care owed by the Ministry of Defence in respect of—

(a)   operations within subsection (2),

(b)   activities carried on in preparation for, or directly in support of, such operations, or

(c)   training of a hazardous nature, or training carried out in a hazardous way, which it is considered needs to be carried out, or carried out in that way, in order to improve or maintain the effectiveness of the armed forces with respect to such operations,

is not a "relevant duty of care".

(2)   The operations within this subsection are operations, including peacekeeping operations and operations for dealing with terrorism, civil unrest or serious public disorder, in the course of which members of the armed forces come under attack or face the threat of attack or violent resistance.

(3)   Any duty of care owed by the Ministry of Defence in respect of activities carried on by members of the special forces is not a "relevant duty of care".

(4)   In this section "the special forces" means those units of the armed forces the maintenance of whose capabilities is the responsibility of the Director of Special Forces or which are for the time being subject to the operational command of that Director.

5   **Policing and law enforcement**

(1)   Any duty of care owed by a public authority in respect of—

(a)   operations within subsection (2),

(b)   activities carried on in preparation for, or directly in support of, such operations, or

(c)   training of a hazardous nature, or training carried out in a hazardous way, which it is considered needs to be carried out, or carried out in that way, in order to improve or maintain the effectiveness of officers or employees of the public authority with respect to such operations,

is not a "relevant duty of care".

(2)   Operations are within this subsection if—

(a)   they are operations for dealing with terrorism, civil unrest or serious disorder,

(b)   they involve the carrying on of policing or law-enforcement activities, and

(c)   officers or employees of the public authority in question come under attack, or face the threat of attack or violent resistance, in the course of the operations.

(3)   Any duty of care owed by a public authority in respect of other policing or law-enforcement activities is not a "relevant duty of care" unless it falls within section 2(1)(a), (b) or (d).

(4)   In this section "policing or law-enforcement activities" includes—

    (a)   activities carried on in the exercise of functions that are—

        (i)   functions of police forces, or

        (ii)   functions of the same or a similar nature exercisable by public authorities other than police forces;

    (b)   activities carried on in the exercise of functions of constables employed by a public authority;

    (c)   activities carried on in the exercise of functions exercisable under Chapter 4 of Part 2 of the Serious Organised Crime and Police Act 2005 (c. 15) (protection of witnesses and other persons);

    (d)   activities carried on to enforce any provision contained in or made under the Immigration Acts.

6   Emergencies

(1)   Any duty of care owed by an organisation within subsection (2) in respect of the way in which it responds to emergency circumstances is not a "relevant duty of care" unless it falls within section 2(1)(a) or (b).

(2)   The organisations within this subsection are—

    (a)   a fire and rescue authority in England and Wales;

    (b)   a fire and rescue authority or joint fire and rescue board in Scotland;

    (c)   the Northern Ireland Fire and Rescue Service Board;

    (d)   any other organisation providing a service of responding to emergency circumstances either—

        (i)   in pursuance of arrangements made with an organisation within paragraph (a), (b) or (c), or

        (ii)   (if not in pursuance of such arrangements) otherwise than on a commercial basis;

    (e)   a relevant NHS body;

    (f)   an organisation providing ambulance services in pursuance of arrangements—

        (i)   made by, or at the request of, a relevant NHS body, or

        (ii)   made with the Secretary of State or with the Welsh Ministers;

    (g)   an organisation providing services for the transport of organs, blood, equipment or personnel in pursuance of arrangements of the kind mentioned in paragraph (f);

(h)   an organisation providing a rescue service;

(i)   the armed forces.

(3)   For the purposes of subsection (1), the way in which an organisation responds to emergency circumstances does not include the way in which—

(a)   medical treatment is carried out, or

(b)   decisions within subsection (4) are made.

(4)   The decisions within this subsection are decisions as to the carrying out of medical treatment, other than decisions as to the order in which persons are to be given such treatment.

(5)   Any duty of care owed in respect of the carrying out, or attempted carrying out, of a rescue operation at sea in emergency circumstances is not a "relevant duty of care" unless it falls within section 2(1)(a) or (b).

(6)   Any duty of care owed in respect of action taken—

(a)   in order to comply with a direction under Schedule 3A to the Merchant Shipping Act 1995 (c. 21) (safety directions), or

(b)   by virtue of paragraph 4 of that Schedule (action in lieu of direction),

is not a "relevant duty of care" unless it falls within section 2(1)(a) or (b).

(7)   In this section—

"emergency circumstances" means circumstances that are present or imminent and—

(a)   are causing, or are likely to cause, serious harm or a worsening of such harm, or

(b)   are likely to cause the death of a person;

"medical treatment" includes any treatment or procedure of a medical or similar nature;

"relevant NHS body" means—

(za)   [the National Health Service Commissioning Board;]

(a)   [a clinical commissioning group,] . . . . Special Health Authority or NHS foundation trust in England;

(b)   a Local Health Board, NHS trust or Special Health Authority in Wales;

(c)   a Health Board or Special Health Board in Scotland, or the Common Services Agency for the Scottish Health Service;

(d)   a Health and Social Services trust or Health and Social Services Board in Northern Ireland;

"serious harm" means—

(a)   serious injury to or the serious illness (including mental illness) of a person;

(b)   serious harm to the environment (including the life and health of plants and animals);

(c)   serious harm to any building or other property.

(8)   A reference in this section to emergency circumstances includes a reference to circumstances that are believed to be emergency circumstances.

7   Child-protection and probation functions

(1)   A duty of care to which this section applies is not a "relevant duty of care" unless it falls within section 2(1)(a), (b) or (d).

(2)   This section applies to any duty of care that a local authority or other public authority owes in respect of the exercise by it of functions conferred by or under—

(a)   Parts 4 and 5 of the Children Act 1989 (c. 41),

(b)   Part 2 of the Children (Scotland) Act 1995 (c. 36), or

(c)   Parts 5 and 6 of the Children (Northern Ireland) Order 1995 (S.I. 1995/755 (N.I. 2)).

(3)   This section also applies to any duty of care that a local probation board [, a provider of probation services] or other public authority owes in respect of the exercise by it of functions conferred by or under—

(a)   Chapter 1 of Part 1 of the Criminal Justice and Court Services Act 2000 (c. 43),

[(aa)   section 13 of the Offender Management Act 2007 (c. 21),]

(b)   section 27 of the Social Work (Scotland) Act 1968 (c. 49), or

(c)   Article 4 of the Probation Board (Northern Ireland) Order 1982 (S.I. 1982/713 (N.I. 10)).

[(4)   This section also applies to any duty of care that a provider of probation services owes in respect of the carrying out by it of activities in pursuance of arrangements under section 3 of the Offender Management Act 2007.]

GROSS BREACH

8   Factors for jury

(1)   This section applies where—

(a)   it is established that an organisation owed a relevant duty of care to a person, and

(b)   it falls to the jury to decide whether there was a gross breach of that duty.

(2)   The jury must consider whether the evidence shows that the organisation failed to comply with any health and safety legislation that relates to the alleged breach, and if so—

(a)   how serious that failure was;

(b)   how much of a risk of death it posed.

(3)   The jury may also—

(a)   consider the extent to which the evidence shows that there were attitudes, policies, systems or accepted practices within the organisation that were likely to have encouraged any such failure as is mentioned in subsection (2), or to have produced tolerance of it;

(b)   have regard to any health and safety guidance that relates to the alleged breach.

(4)   This section does not prevent the jury from having regard to any other matters they consider relevant.

(5)   In this section "health and safety guidance" means any code, guidance, manual or similar publication that is concerned with health and safety matters and is made or issued (under a statutory provision or otherwise) by an authority responsible for the enforcement of any health and safety legislation.

REMEDIAL ORDERS AND PUBLICITY ORDERS

9   **Power to order breach etc to be remedied**

(1)   A court before which an organisation is convicted of corporate manslaughter or corporate homicide may make an order (a "remedial order") requiring the organisation to take specified steps to remedy—

(a)   the breach mentioned in section 1(1) ("the relevant breach");

(b)   any matter that appears to the court to have resulted from the relevant breach and to have been a cause of the death;

(c)   any deficiency, as regards health and safety matters, in the organisation's policies, systems or practices of which the relevant breach appears to the court to be an indication.

(2)   A remedial order may be made only on an application by the prosecution specifying the terms of the proposed order.
Any such order must be on such terms (whether those proposed or others) as the court considers appropriate having regard to any representations made, and any evidence adduced, in relation to that matter by the prosecution or on behalf of the organisation.

(3)   Before making an application for a remedial order the prosecution must consult such enforcement authority or authorities as it considers appropriate having regard to the nature of the relevant breach.

(4)   A remedial order—

(a)   must specify a period within which the steps referred to in subsection (1) are to be taken;

(b)   may require the organisation to supply to an enforcement authority consulted under subsection (3), within a specified period, evidence that those steps have been taken.

A period specified under this subsection may be extended or further extended by order of the court on an application made before the end of that period or extended period.

(5) An organisation that fails to comply with a remedial order is guilty of an offence, and liable on conviction on indictment to a fine.

10 Power to order conviction etc to be publicised

(1) A court before which an organisation is convicted of corporate manslaughter or corporate homicide may make an order (a "publicity order") requiring the organisation to publicise in a specified manner—

(a) the fact that it has been convicted of the offence;

(b) specified particulars of the offence;

(c) the amount of any fine imposed;

(d) the terms of any remedial order made.

(2) In deciding on the terms of a publicity order that it is proposing to make, the court must—

(a) ascertain the views of such enforcement authority or authorities (if any) as it considers appropriate, and

(b) have regard to any representations made by the prosecution or on behalf of the organisation.

(3) A publicity order—

(a) must specify a period within which the requirements referred to in subsection (1) are to be complied with;

(b) may require the organisation to supply to any enforcement authority whose views have been ascertained under subsection (2), within a specified period, evidence that those requirements have been complied with.

(4) An organisation that fails to comply with a publicity order is guilty of an offence, and liable on conviction on indictment to a fine.

APPLICATION TO PARTICULAR CATEGORIES OF ORGANISATION

11 Application to Crown bodies

(1) An organisation that is a servant or agent of the Crown is not immune from prosecution under this Act for that reason.

(2) For the purposes of this Act—

(a) a department or other body listed in Schedule 1, or

(b) a corporation that is a servant or agent of the Crown,

is to be treated as owing whatever duties of care it would owe if it were a corporation that was not a servant or agent of the Crown.

(3) For the purposes of section 2—

(a) a person who is—

> > (i)   employed by or under the Crown for the purposes of a department or other body listed in Schedule 1, or
> >
> > (ii)   employed by a person whose staff constitute a body listed in that Schedule,
> >
> > is to be treated as employed by that department or body;
> >
> > (b)   any premises occupied for the purposes of—
> >
> > (i)   a department or other body listed in Schedule 1, or
> >
> > (ii)   a person whose staff constitute a body listed in that Schedule,
> >
> > are to be treated as occupied by that department or body.
>
> (4)   For the purposes of sections 2 to 7 anything done purportedly by a department or other body listed in Schedule 1, although in law by the Crown or by the holder of a particular office, is to be treated as done by the department or other body itself.
>
> (5)   Subsections (3)(a)(i), (3)(b)(i) and (4) apply in relation to a Northern Ireland department as they apply in relation to a department or other body listed in Schedule 1.

12   Application to armed forces

> (1)   In this Act "the armed forces" means any of the naval, military or air forces of the Crown raised under the law of the United Kingdom.
>
> (2)   For the purposes of section 2 a person who is a member of the armed forces is to be treated as employed by the Ministry of Defence.
>
> (3)   A reference in this Act to members of the armed forces includes a reference to—
>
> > (a)   members of the reserve forces (within the meaning given by section 1(2) of the Reserve Forces Act 1996 (c. 14)) when in service or undertaking training or duties;
> >
> > (b)   persons serving on Her Majesty's vessels (within the meaning given by section 132(1) of the Naval Discipline Act 1957 (c. 53)).

13   Application to police forces

> (1)   In this Act "police force" means—
>
> > (a)   a police force within the meaning of—
> >
> > (i)   the Police Act 1996 (c. 16), or
> >
> > (ii)   the Police (Scotland) Act 1967 (c. 77);
> >
> > (b)   the Police Service of Northern Ireland;
> >
> > (c)   the Police Service of Northern Ireland Reserve;
> >
> > (d)   the British Transport Police Force;
> >
> > (e)   the Civil Nuclear Constabulary;
> >
> > (f)   the Ministry of Defence Police.

(2)   For the purposes of this Act a police force is to be treated as owing whatever duties of care it would owe if it were a body corporate.

(3)   For the purposes of section 2—

(a)   a member of a police force is to be treated as employed by that force;

(b)   a special constable appointed for a police area in England and Wales is to be treated as employed by the police force maintained by the [local policing body] for that area;

(c)   a special constable appointed for a police force mentioned in paragraph (d) or (f) of subsection (1) is to be treated as employed by that force;

(d)   a police cadet undergoing training with a view to becoming a member of a police force mentioned in paragraph (a) or (d) of subsection (1) is to be treated as employed by that force;

(e)   a police trainee appointed under section 39 of the Police (Northern Ireland) Act 2000 (c. 32) or a police cadet appointed under section 42 of that Act is to be treated as employed by the Police Service of Northern Ireland;

(f)   a police reserve trainee appointed under section 40 of that Act is to be treated as employed by the Police Service of Northern Ireland Reserve;

(g)   a member of a police force seconded to the Serious Organised Crime Agency or the National Policing Improvement Agency to serve as a member of its staff is to be treated as employed by that Agency.

(4)   A reference in subsection (3) to a member of a police force is to be read, in the case of a force mentioned in paragraph (a)(ii) of subsection (1), as a reference to a constable of that force.

(5)   For the purposes of section 2 any premises occupied for the purposes of a police force are to be treated as occupied by that force.

(6)   For the purposes of sections 2 to 7 anything that would be regarded as done by a police force if the force were a body corporate is to be so regarded.

(7)   Where—

(a)   by virtue of subsection (3) a person is treated for the purposes of section 2 as employed by a police force, and

(b)   by virtue of any other statutory provision (whenever made) he is, or is treated as, employed by another organisation,

the person is to be treated for those purposes as employed by both the force and the other organisation.

14   **Application to partnerships**

(1)   For the purposes of this Act a partnership is to be treated as owing whatever duties of care it would owe if it were a body corporate.

(2)   Proceedings for an offence under this Act alleged to have been committed by

a partnership are to be brought in the name of the partnership (and not in that of any of its members).

(3)   A fine imposed on a partnership on its conviction of an offence under this Act is to be paid out of the funds of the partnership.

(4)   This section does not apply to a partnership that is a legal person under the law by which it is governed.

MISCELLANEOUS

17   **DPP's consent required for proceedings**

Proceedings for an offence of corporate manslaughter—

(a)   may not be instituted in England and Wales without the consent of the Director of Public Prosecutions;

(b)   may not be instituted in Northern Ireland without the consent of the Director of Public Prosecutions for Northern Ireland.

18   **No individual liability**

(1)   An individual cannot be guilty of aiding, abetting, counselling or procuring the commission of an offence of corporate manslaughter.

[(1A)   An individual cannot be guilty of an offence under Part 2 of the Serious Crime Act 2007 (encouraging or assisting crime) by reference to an offence of corporate manslaughter.]

(2)   An individual cannot be guilty of aiding, abetting, counselling or procuring, or being art and part in, the commission of an offence of corporate homicide.

19   **Convictions under this Act and under health and safety legislation**

(1)   Where in the same proceedings there is—

(a)   a charge of corporate manslaughter or corporate homicide arising out of a particular set of circumstances, and

(b)   a charge against the same defendant of a health and safety offence arising out of some or all of those circumstances,

the jury may, if the interests of justice so require, be invited to return a verdict on each charge.

(2)   An organisation that has been convicted of corporate manslaughter or corporate homicide arising out of a particular set of circumstances may, if the interests of justice so require, be charged with a health and safety offence arising out of some or all of those circumstances.

(3)   In this section "health and safety offence" means an offence under any health and safety legislation.

20   **Abolition of liability of corporations for manslaughter at common law**

The common law offence of manslaughter by gross negligence is abolished in its application to corporations, and in any application it has to other organisations to which section 1 applies.

GENERAL AND SUPPLEMENTAL

25   Interpretation

In this Act—

"armed forces" has the meaning given by section 12(1);

"corporation" does not include a corporation sole but includes any body corporate wherever incorporated;

"employee" means an individual who works under a contract of employment or apprenticeship (whether express or implied and, if express, whether oral or in writing), and related expressions are to be construed accordingly; see also sections 11(3)(a), 12(2) and 13(3) (which apply for the purposes of section 2);

"employers' association" has the meaning given by section 122 of the Trade Union and Labour Relations (Consolidation) Act 1992 (c. 52) or Article 4 of the Industrial Relations (Northern Ireland) Order 1992 (S.I. 1992/807 (N.I. 5));

"enforcement authority" means an authority responsible for the enforcement of any health and safety legislation;

"health and safety legislation" means any statutory provision dealing with health and safety matters, including in particular provision contained in the Health and Safety at Work etc. Act 1974 (c. 37) or the Health and Safety at Work (Northern Ireland) Order 1978 (S.I. 1978/1039 (N.I. 9));

"member", in relation to the armed forces, is to be read in accordance with section 12(3);

"partnership" means—

(a)   a partnership within the Partnership Act 1890 (c. 39), or

(b)   a limited partnership registered under the Limited Partnerships Act 1907 (c. 24),

or a firm or entity of a similar character formed under the law of a country or territory outside the United Kingdom;

"police force" has the meaning given by section 13(1);

"premises" includes land, buildings and moveable structures;

"public authority" has the same meaning as in section 6 of the Human Rights Act 1998 (c. 42) (disregarding subsections (3)(a) and (4) of that section);

"publicity order" means an order under section 10(1);

"remedial order" means an order under section 9(1);

"statutory provision", except in section 15, means provision contained in, or in an instrument made under, any Act, any Act of the Scottish Parliament or any Northern Ireland legislation;

"trade union" has the meaning given by section 1 of the Trade Union and Labour

Relations (Consolidation) Act 1992 (c. 52) or Article 3 of the Industrial Relations (Northern Ireland) Order 1992 (S.I. 1992/807 (N.I. 5)).

28   **Extent and territorial application**

(1)   Subject to subsection (2), this Act extends to England and Wales, Scotland and Northern Ireland.

(2)   An amendment made by this Act extends to the same part or parts of the United Kingdom as the provision to which it relates.

(3)   Section 1 applies if the harm resulting in death is sustained in the United Kingdom or—

    (a)   within the seaward limits of the territorial sea adjacent to the United Kingdom;

    (b)   on a ship registered under Part 2 of the Merchant Shipping Act 1995 (c. 21);

    (c)   on a British-controlled aircraft as defined in section 92 of the Civil Aviation Act 1982 (c. 16);

    (d)   on a British-controlled hovercraft within the meaning of that section as applied in relation to hovercraft by virtue of provision made under the Hovercraft Act 1968 (c. 59);

    (e)   in any place to which an Order in Council under section 10(1) of the Petroleum Act 1998 (c. 17) applies (criminal jurisdiction in relation to offshore activities).

(4)   For the purposes of subsection (3)(b) to (d) harm sustained on a ship, aircraft or hovercraft includes harm sustained by a person who—

    (a)   is then no longer on board the ship, aircraft or hovercraft in consequence of the wrecking of it or of some other mishap affecting it or occurring on it, and

    (b)   sustains the harm in consequence of that event.

SCHEDULE 1
LIST OF GOVERNMENT DEPARTMENTS ETC
SECTION 1

. . . .

Attorney General's Office

Cabinet Office

Central Office of Information

Crown Office and Procurator Fiscal Service

Crown Prosecution Service

. . . .

. . . .

[Department for Business, Innovation and Skills]

Department for Communities and Local Government

. . . .

Department for Culture, Media and Sport

. . . .

[Department for Education]

Department for Environment, Food and Rural Affairs

. . . .

Department for International Development

Department for Transport

Department for Work and Pensions

[Department of Energy and Climate Change]

Department of Health

. . . .

Export Credits Guarantee Department

Foreign and Commonwealth Office

Forestry Commission

General Register Office for Scotland

Government Actuary's Department

Her Majesty's Land Registry

Her Majesty's Revenue and Customs

Her Majesty's Treasury

Home Office

[Ministry of Justice (including the Scotland Office and the Wales Office)]

Ministry of Defence

National Archives

National Archives of Scotland

[. . . . .]

National Savings and Investments

National School of Government

Northern Ireland Audit Office

. . . .

Northern Ireland Office

Office for National Statistics

. . . .

Office of Her Majesty's Chief Inspector of Education and Training in Wales

Ordnance Survey

. . . .

Public Prosecution Service for Northern Ireland

Registers of Scotland Executive Agency

Revenue and Customs Prosecutions Office

Royal Mint

Scottish Executive

Serious Fraud Office

Treasury Solicitor's Department

UK Trade and Investment

Welsh Assembly Government

SCHEDULE 2
MINOR AND CONSEQUENTIAL AMENDMENTS
SECTION 26

1   **Coroners Act 1988 (c. 13)**

      . . . .

2   **Criminal Justice Act 2003 (c. 44)**

In Schedule 4 to the Criminal Justice Act 2003 (qualifying offences for purposes of section 62), after paragraph 4 there is inserted—

"4A   **Corporate manslaughter**

An offence under section 1 of the Corporate Manslaughter and Corporate Homicide Act 2007."

3   (1)   Schedule 5 to that Act (qualifying offences for purposes of Part 10) is amended as follows.

      (2)   After paragraph 4 there is inserted—

"4A   **Corporate manslaughter**

An offence under section 1 of the Corporate Manslaughter and Corporate Homicide Act 2007."

      (3)   After paragraph 33 there is inserted—

"33A   **Corporate manslaughter**

An offence under section 1 of the Corporate Manslaughter and Corporate Homicide Act 2007."

4   **Criminal Justice (Northern Ireland) Order 2004 (S.I. 2004/1500 (N.I. 9))**

In Schedule 2 to the Criminal Justice (Northern Ireland) Order 2004 (qualifying offences for purposes of Article 21), after paragraph 4 there is inserted—

"4A   Corporate manslaughter

An offence under section 1 of the Corporate Manslaughter and Corporate Homicide Act 2007."

Criminal Justice and Immigration Act 2008

2008 c. 4

PART 5
CRIMINAL LAW

SELF-DEFENCE ETC.

76   Reasonable force for purposes of self-defence etc.

(1)   This section applies where in proceedings for an offence—

(a)   an issue arises as to whether a person charged with the offence ("D") is entitled to rely on a defence within subsection (2), and

(b)   the question arises whether the degree of force used by D against a person ("V") was reasonable in the circumstances.

(2)   The defences are—

(a)   the common law defence of self-defence; . . .

[(aa)   the common law defence of defence of property; and]

(b)   the defences provided by section 3(1) of the Criminal Law Act 1967 (c. 58) or section 3(1) of the Criminal Law Act (Northern Ireland) 1967 (c. 18 (N.I.)) (use of force in prevention of crime or making arrest).

(3)   The question whether the degree of force used by D was reasonable in the circumstances is to be decided by reference to the circumstances as D believed them to be, and subsections (4) to (8) also apply in connection with deciding that question.

(4)   If D claims to have held a particular belief as regards the existence of any circumstances—

(a)   the reasonableness or otherwise of that belief is relevant to the question whether D genuinely held it; but

(b)   if it is determined that D did genuinely hold it, D is entitled to rely on it for the purposes of subsection (3), whether or not—

(i)   it was mistaken, or

(ii)   (if it was mistaken) the mistake was a reasonable one to have made.

(5)   But subsection (4)(b) does not enable D to rely on any mistaken belief attributable to intoxication that was voluntarily induced.

(6)   The degree of force used by D is not to be regarded as having been reasonable in the circumstances as D believed them to be if it was disproportionate in those circumstances.

[(6A)   In deciding the question mentioned in subsection (3), a possibility that D could have retreated is to be considered (so far as relevant) as a factor to be taken into account, rather than as giving rise to a duty to retreat.]

(7)   In deciding the question mentioned in subsection (3) the following considerations are to be taken into account (so far as relevant in the circumstances of the case)—

   (a)   that a person acting for a legitimate purpose may not be able to weigh to a nicety the exact measure of any necessary action; and

   (b)   that evidence of a person's having only done what the person honestly and instinctively thought was necessary for a legitimate purpose constitutes strong evidence that only reasonable action was taken by that person for that purpose.

(8)   [Subsections (6A) and (7) are] not to be read as preventing other matters from being taken into account where they are relevant to deciding the question mentioned in subsection (3).

(9)   This section is intended to clarify the operation of the existing defences mentioned in subsection (2).

(10)   In this section—

   (a)   "legitimate purpose" means—

      (i)   the purpose of self-defence under the common law, . . .

      [(ia)   the purpose of defence of property under the common law, or]

      (ii)   the prevention of crime or effecting or assisting in the lawful arrest of persons mentioned in the provisions referred to in subsection (2)(b);

   (b)   references to self-defence include acting in defence of another person; and

   (c)   references to the degree of force used are to the type and amount of force used.

Criminal Law Act 1967

1967 c. 58

PART I
FELONY AND MISDEMEANOUR

1 **Abolition of distinction between felony and misdemeanour.**

(1) All distinctions between felony and misdemeanour are hereby abolished.

(2) Subject to the provisions of this Act, on all matters on which a distinction has previously been made between felony and misdemeanour, including mode of trial, the law and practice in relation to all offences cognisable under the law of England and Wales (including piracy) shall be the law and practice applicable at the commencement of this Act in relation to misdemeanour.

3 **Use of force in making arrest, etc.**

(1) A person may use such force as is reasonable in the circumstances in the prevention of crime, or in effecting or assisting in the lawful arrest of offenders or suspected offenders or of persons unlawfully at large.

(2) Subsection (1) above shall replace the rules of the common law on the question when force used for a purpose mentioned in the subsection is justified by that purpose.

4 **Penalties for assisting offenders.**

(1) Where a person has committed [a relevant offence], any other person who, knowing or believing him to be guilty of the offence or of some [other relevant offence], does without lawful authority or reasonable excuse any act with intent to impede his apprehension or prosecution shall be guilty of an offence.

[(1A) In this section and section 5 below, relevant offence means—

(a) an offence for which the sentence is fixed by law,

(b) an offence for which a person of 18 years or over (not previously convicted) may be sentenced to imprisonment for a term of five years (or might be so sentenced but for the restrictions imposed by section 33 of the Magistrates' Courts Act 1980).]

(2) If on the trial of an indictment for [a relevant offence] the jury are satisfied that the offence charged (or some other offence of which the accused might on that charge be found guilty) was committed, but find the accused not guilty of it, they may find him guilty of any offence under subsection (1) above of which they are satisfied that he is guilty in relation to the offence charged (or that other offence).

(3) A person committing an offence under subsection (1) above with intent to

impede another person's apprehension or prosecution shall on conviction on indictment be liable to imprisonment according to the gravity of the other person's offence, as follows:—

(a) if that offence is one for which the sentence is fixed by law, he shall be liable to imprisonment for not more than ten years;

(b) if it is one for which a person (not previously convicted) may be sentenced to imprisonment for a term of fourteen years, he shall be liable to imprisonment for not more than seven years;

(c) if it is not one included above but is one for which a person (not previously convicted) may be sentenced to imprisonment for a term of ten years, he shall be liable to imprisonment for not more than five years;

(d) in any other case, he shall be liable to imprisonment for not more than three years.

(4) No proceedings shall be instituted for an offence under subsection (1) above except by or with the consent of the Director of Public Prosecutions: . . .

(5) . . . .

(6) . . . .

(7) . . . .

5   Penalties for concealing offences or giving false information.

(1) Where a person has committed [a relevant offence], any other person who, knowing or believing that the offence or some [other relevant offence] has been committed, and that he has information which might be of material assistance in securing the prosecution or conviction of an offender for it, accepts or agrees to accept for not disclosing that information any consideration other than the making good of loss or injury caused by the offence, or the making of reasonable compensation for that loss or injury, shall be liable on conviction on indictment to imprisonment for not more that two years.

(2) Where a person causes any wasteful employment of the police by knowingly making to any person a false report tending to show that an offence has been committed, or to give rise to apprehension for the safety of any persons or property, or tending to show that he has information material to any police inquiry, he shall be liable on summary conviction to imprisonment for not more than six months or to a fine of not more than two hundred pounds or to both.

(3) No proceedings shall be instituted for an offence under this section except by or with the consent of the Director of Public Prosecutions.

(4) . . . .

(5) The compounding of an offence other than treason shall not be an offence otherwise than under this section.

6   **Trial of offences.**

(1)   Where a person is arraigned on an indictment—

(a)   he shall in all cases be entitled to make a plea of not guilty in addition to any demurrer or special plea;

(b)   he may plead not guilty of the offence specifically charged in the indictment but guilty of another offence of which he might be found guilty on that indictment;

(c)   if he stands mute of malice or will not answer directly to the indictment, the court may order a plea of not guilty to be entered on his behalf, and he shall then be treated as having pleaded not guilty.

(2)   On an indictment for murder a person found not guilty of murder may be found guilty—

(a)   of manslaughter, or of causing grievous bodily harm with intent to do so; or

(b)   of any offence of which he may be found guilty under an enactment specifically so providing, or under section 4(2) of this Act; or

(c)   of an attempt to commit murder, or of an attempt to commit any other offence of which he might be found guilty;

but may not be found guilty of any offence not included above.

(3)   Where, on a person's trial on indictment for any offence except treason or murder, the jury find him not guilty of the offence specifically charged in the indictment, but the allegations in the indictment amount to or include (expressly or by implication) an allegation of another offence falling within the jurisdiction of the court of trial, the jury may find him guilty of that other offence or of an offence of which he could be found guilty on an indictment specifically charging that other offence.

[(3A)   For the purposes of subsection (3) above an offence falls within the jurisdiction of the court of trial if it is an offence to which section 40 of the Criminal Justice Act 1988 applies (power to join in indictment count for common assault etc.), even if a count charging the offence is not included in the indictment

(3B)   A person convicted of an offence by virtue of subsection (3A) may only be dealt with for it in a manner in which a magistrates' court could have dealt with him.]

(4)   For purposes of subsection (3) above any allegation of an offence shall be taken as including an allegation of attempting to commit that offence; and where a person is charged on indictment with attempting to commit an offence or with any assault or other act preliminary to an offence, but not with the completed offence, then (subject to the discretion of the court to discharge the jury [or otherwise act] with a view to the preferment of an indictment for the completed offence) he may be convicted of the offence charged notwithstanding that he is shown to be guilty of the completed offence.

(5)   Where a person arraigned on an indictment pleads not guilty of an offence charged in the indictment but guilty of some other offence of which he might be found guilty on that charge, and he is convicted on that plea of guilty without trial for the offence of which he has pleaded not guilty, then (whether or not the two offences are separately charged in distinct counts) his conviction of the one offence shall be an acquittal of the other.

(6)   Any power to bring proceedings for an offence by criminal information in the High Court is hereby abolished.

(7)   Subsections (1) to (3) above shall apply to an indictment containing more than one count as if each count were a separate indictment.

Criminal Law Act 1977

1977 c. 45

PART II
OFFENCES RELATING TO ENTERING
AND REMAINING ON PROPERTY

9   **Trespassing on premises of foreign missions, etc.**

(1)   Subject to subsection (3) below, a person who enters or is on any premises to which this section applies as a trespasser is guilty of an offence.

(2)   This section applies to any premises which are or form part of—

(a)   the premises of a diplomatic mission within the meaning of the definition in Article 1(*i*) of the Vienna Convention on Diplomatic Relations signed in 1961 as that Article has effect in the United Kingdom by virtue of section 2 of and Schedule 1 to the Diplomatic Privileges Act 1964;

[(aa)   the premises of a closed diplomatic mission;]

(b)   consular premises within the meaning of the definition in paragraph 1(*j*) of Article 1 of the Vienna Convention on Consular Relations signed in 1963 as that Article has effect in the United Kingdom by virtue of section 1 of and Schedule 1 to the Consular Relations Act 1968;

[(bb)   the premises of a closed consular post;]

(c)   any other premises in respect of which any organisation or body is entitled to inviolability by or under any enactment; and

(d)   any premises which are the private residence of a diplomatic agent (within the meaning of Article 1(*e*) of the Convention mentioned in paragraph (*a*) above) or of any other person who is entitled to inviolability of residence by or under any enactment.

[(2A) In subsection (2) above—

"the premises of a closed diplomatic mission" means premises which fall within Article 45 of the Convention mentioned in subsection (2)(a) above (as that Article has effect in the United Kingdom by virtue of the section and Schedule mentioned in that paragraph); and

"the premises of a closed consular post" means premises which fall within Article 27 of the Convention mentioned in subsection (2)(b) above (as that Article has effect in the United Kingdom by virtue of the section and Schedule mentioned in that paragraph);]

(3) In any proceedings for an offence under this section it shall be a defence for the accused to prove that he believed that the premises in question were not premises to which this section applies.

(4) In any proceedings for an offence under this section a certificate issued by or under the authority of the Secretary of State stating that any premises were or formed part of premises of any description mentioned in paragraphs (a) to (d) of subsection (2) above at the time of the alleged offence shall be conclusive evidence that the premises were or formed part of premises of that description at that time.

(5) A person guilty of an offence under this section shall be liable on summary conviction to imprisonment for a term not exceeding six months or to a fine not exceeding [level 5 on the standard scale] or to both.

(6) Proceedings for an offence under this section shall not be instituted against any person except by or with the consent of the Attorney General.

(7) . . . .

Criminal Procedure (Insanity) Act 1964

1964 c. 84

[4 **Finding of unfitness to plead.**

(1) This section applies where on the trial of a person the question arises (at the instance of the defence or otherwise) whether the accused is under a disability, that is to say, under any disability such that apart from this Act it would constitute a bar to his being tried.

(2) If, having regard to the nature of the supposed disability, the court are of opinion that it is expedient to do so and in the interests of the accused, they may postpone consideration of the question of fitness to be tried until any time up to the opening of the case for the defence.

(3) If, before the question of fitness to be tried falls to be determined, the jury return a verdict of acquittal on the count or each of the counts on which the accused is being tried, that question shall not be determined.

(4) Subject to subsections (2) and (3) above, the question of fitness to be tried

shall be determined as soon as it arises.

(5)   [Where the question of disability was determined after arraignment of the accused, the determination under subsection (2) is to be made by the jury by whom he was being tried.]

(6)   [The court] shall not make a determination under subsection (5) above except on the written or oral evidence of two or more registered medical practitioners at least one of whom is duly approved.]

4A   **Finding that the accused did the act or made the omission charged against him.**

(1)   This section applies where in accordance with section 4(5) above it is determined by a [court] that the accused is under a disability.

(2)   The trial shall not proceed or further proceed but it shall be determined by a jury—

    (a)   on the evidence (if any) already given in the trial; and

    (b)   on such evidence as may be adduced or further adduced by the prosecution, or adduced by a person appointed by the court under this section to put the case for the defence,

whether they are satisfied, as respects the count or each of the counts on which the accused was to be or was being tried, that he did the act or made the omission charged against him as the offence.

(3)   If as respects that count or any of those counts the jury are satisfied as mentioned in subsection (2) above, they shall make a finding that the accused did the act or made the omission charged against him.

(4)   If as respects that count or any of those counts the jury are not so satisfied, they shall return a verdict of acquittal as if on the count in question the trial had proceeded to a conclusion.

(5)   A determination under subsection (2) above shall be made—

    (a)   where the question of disability was determined on the arraignment of the accused, by a jury other than that which determined that question; and

    (b)   where that question was determined at any later time, by the jury by whom the accused was being tried.

[5   **Powers to deal with persons not guilty by reason of insanity or unfit to plead etc**

(1)   This section applies where—

    (a)   a special verdict is returned that the accused is not guilty by reason of insanity; or

    (b)   findings have been made that the accused is under a disability and that he did the act or made the omission charged against him.

(2)   The court shall make in respect of the accused—

    (a)   a hospital order (with or without a restriction order);

      (b)   a supervision order; or

      (c)   an order for his absolute discharge.

(3)   Where—

      (a)   the offence to which the special verdict or the findings relate is an offence the sentence for which is fixed by law, and

      (b)   the court have power to make a hospital order,

the court shall make a hospital order with a restriction order (whether or not they would have power to make a restriction order apart from this subsection).

(4)   In this section—

"hospital order" has the meaning given in section 37 of the Mental Health Act 1983;

"restriction order" has the meaning given to it by section 41 of that Act;

"supervision order" has the meaning given in Part 1 of Schedule 1A to this Act.]

[5A   Orders made under or by virtue of section 5

(1)   In relation to the making of an order by virtue of subsection (2)(a) of section 5 above, section 37 (hospital orders etc) of the Mental Health Act 1983 ("the 1983 Act") shall have effect as if—

      (a)   the reference in subsection (1) to a person being convicted before the Crown Court included a reference to the case where section 5 above applies;

      (b)   the words after "punishable with imprisonment" and before "or is convicted" were omitted; and

      (c)   for subsections (4) and (5) there were substituted—

(4) Where an order is made under this section requiring a person to be admitted to a hospital ("a hospital order"), it shall be the duty of the managers of the hospital specified in the order to admit him in accordance with it.

(2)   In relation to a case where section 5 above applies but the court have not yet made one of the disposals mentioned in subsection (2) of that section—

      (a)   section 35 of the 1983 Act (remand to hospital for report on accused's mental condition) shall have effect with the omission of the words after paragraph (b) in subsection (3);

      (b)   section 36 of that Act (remand of accused person to hospital for treatment) shall have effect with the omission of the words "(other than an offence the sentence for which is fixed by law)" in subsection (2);

      (c)   references in sections 35 and 36 of that Act to an accused person shall be construed as including a person in whose case this subsection applies; and

(d)   section 38 of that Act (interim hospital orders) shall have effect as if
—

    (i)   the reference in subsection (1) to a person being convicted before the Crown Court included a reference to the case where section 5 above applies; and

    (ii)   the words "(other than an offence the sentence for which is fixed by law)" in that subsection were omitted.

(3)   In relation to the making of any order under the 1983 Act by virtue of this Act, references in the 1983 Act to an offender shall be construed as including references to a person in whose case section 5 above applies, and references to an offence shall be construed accordingly.

(4)   Where—

(a)   a person is detained in pursuance of a hospital order which the court had power to make by virtue of section 5(1)(b) above, and

(b)   the court also made a restriction order, and that order has not ceased to have effect,

the Secretary of State, if satisfied after consultation with the [the responsible clinician] that the person can properly be tried, may remit the person for trial, either to the court of trial or to a prison.

On the person's arrival at the court or prison, the hospital order and the restriction order shall cease to have effect.

(5)   Schedule 1A to this Act (supervision orders) has effect with respect to the making of supervision orders under subsection (2)(b) of section 5 above, and with respect to the revocation and amendment of such orders.

(6)   In relation to the making of an order under subsection (2)(c) of section 5 above, section 12(1) of the Powers of Criminal Courts (Sentencing) Act 2000 (absolute and conditional discharge) shall have effect as if—

(a)   the reference to a person being convicted by or before a court of such an offence as is there mentioned included a reference to the case where section 5 above applies; and

(b)   the reference to the court being of opinion that it is inexpedient to inflict punishment included a reference to it thinking that an order for absolute discharge would be most suitable in all the circumstances of the case.]

6   **Evidence by prosecution of insanity or diminished responsibility.**

Where on a trial for murder the accused contends—

(a)   that at the time of the alleged offence he was insane so as not to be responsible according to law for his actions; or

(b)   that at that time he was suffering from such abnormality of [mental functioning] as is specified in subsection (1) of section 2 of the Homicide Act

1957 (diminished responsibility),

the court shall allow the prosecution to adduce or elicit evidence tending to prove the other of those contentions, and may give directions as to the stage of the proceedings at which the prosecution may adduce such evidence.

2, 3.   . . . .

Criminal Procedure (Insanity and Unfitness to Plead) Act 1991

1991 c. 25

1   **Acquittals on grounds of insanity.**

(1)   A jury shall not return a special verdict under section 2 of the Trial of Lunatics Act 1883 (acquittal on ground of insanity) except on the written or oral evidence of two or more registered medical practitioners at least one of whom is duly approved.

(2)   Subsections (2) and (3) of section 54 of the Mental Health Act 1983 ("the 1983 Act") shall have effect with respect to proof of the accused's mental condition for the purposes of the said section 2 as they have effect with respect to proof of an offender's mental condition for the purposes of section 37(2)(a) of that Act.

6   **Interpretation etc.**

(1)   In this Act—

"the 1964 Act" means the Criminal Procedure (Insanity) Act 1964;

"the 1968 Act" means the Criminal Appeal Act 1968;

"the 1983 Act" means the Mental Health Act 1983;

"duly approved", in relation to a registered medical practitioner, means approved for the purposes of section 12 of the 1983 Act by the Secretary of State as having special experience in the diagnosis or treatment of mental disorder.

. . . .

(2)   . . . .

.2   **Findings of unfitness to plead etc.**

For section 4 of the Criminal Procedure (Insanity) Act 1964 ("the 1964 Act") there shall be substituted the following sections—

"4   **Finding of unfitness to plead.**

(1)   This section applies where on the trial of a person the question arises (at

the instance of the defence or otherwise) whether the accused is under a disability, that is to say, under any disability such that apart from this Act it would constitute a bar to his being tried.

(2)   If, having regard to the nature of the supposed disability, the court are of opinion that it is expedient to do so and in the interests of the accused, they may postpone consideration of the question of fitness to be tried until any time up to the opening of the case for the defence.

(3)   If, before the question of fitness to be tried falls to be determined, the jury return a verdict of acquittal on the count or each of the counts on which the accused is being tried, that question shall not be determined.

(4)   Subject to subsections (2) and (3) above, the question of fitness to be tried shall be determined as soon as it arises.

(5)   The question of fitness to be tried shall be determined by a jury and—

    (a)   where it falls to be determined on the arraignment of the accused and the trial proceeds, the accused shall be tried by a jury other than that which determined that question;

    (b)   where it falls to be determined at any later time, it shall be determined by a separate jury or by the jury by whom the accused is being tried, as the court may direct.

(6)   A jury shall not make a determination under subsection (5) above except on the written or oral evidence of two or more registered medical practitioners at least one of whom is duly approved.

4A   **Finding that the accused did the act or made the omission charged against him.**

(1)   This section applies where in accordance with section 4(5) above it is determined by a jury that the accused is under a disability.

(2)   The trial shall not proceed or further proceed but it shall be determined by a jury—

    (a)   on the evidence (if any) already given in the trial; and

    (b)   on such evidence as may be adduced or further adduced by the prosecution, or adduced by a person appointed by the court under this section to put the case for the defence,

whether they are satisfied, as respects the count or each of the counts on which the accused was to be or was being tried, that he did the act or made the omission charged against him as the offence.

(3)   If as respects that count or any of those counts the jury are satisfied as mentioned in subsection (2) above, they shall make a finding that the accused did the act or made the omission charged against him.

(4)   If as respects that count or any of those counts the jury are not so satisfied, they shall return a verdict of acquittal as if on the count in question the trial had proceeded to a conclusion.

(5)   A determination under subsection (2) above shall be made—

(a)   where the question of disability was determined on the arraignment of the accused, by a jury other than that which determined that question; and

(b)   where that question was determined at any later time, by the jury by whom the accused was being tried."

Fraud Act 2006

2006 c. 35

FRAUD

1   **Fraud**

(1)   A person is guilty of fraud if he is in breach of any of the sections listed in subsection (2) (which provide for different ways of committing the offence).

(2)   The sections are—

(a)   section 2 (fraud by false representation),

(b)   section 3 (fraud by failing to disclose information), and

(c)   section 4 (fraud by abuse of position).

(3)   A person who is guilty of fraud is liable—

(a)   on summary conviction, to imprisonment for a term not exceeding 12 months or to a fine not exceeding the statutory maximum (or to both);

(b)   on conviction on indictment, to imprisonment for a term not exceeding 10 years or to a fine (or to both).

(4)   Subsection (3)(a) applies in relation to Northern Ireland as if the reference to 12 months were a reference to 6 months.

2   **Fraud by false representation**

(1)   A person is in breach of this section if he—

(a)   dishonestly makes a false representation, and

(b)   intends, by making the representation—

(i)   to make a gain for himself or another, or

(ii)   to cause loss to another or to expose another to a risk of loss.

(2)   A representation is false if—

(a)   it is untrue or misleading, and

(b)   the person making it knows that it is, or might be, untrue or misleading.

(3)   "Representation" means any representation as to fact or law, including a

representation as to the state of mind of—

(a)   the person making the representation, or

(b)   any other person.

(4)   A representation may be express or implied.

(5)   For the purposes of this section a representation may be regarded as made if it (or anything implying it) is submitted in any form to any system or device designed to receive, convey or respond to communications (with or without human intervention).

3 Fraud by failing to disclose information

A person is in breach of this section if he—

(a)   dishonestly fails to disclose to another person information which he is under a legal duty to disclose, and

(b)   intends, by failing to disclose the information—

(i)   to make a gain for himself or another, or

(ii)   to cause loss to another or to expose another to a risk of loss.

4 Fraud by abuse of position

(1)   A person is in breach of this section if he—

(a)   occupies a position in which he is expected to safeguard, or not to act against, the financial interests of another person,

(b)   dishonestly abuses that position, and

(c)   intends, by means of the abuse of that position—

(i)   to make a gain for himself or another, or

(ii)   to cause loss to another or to expose another to a risk of loss.

(2)   A person may be regarded as having abused his position even though his conduct consisted of an omission rather than an act.

5 "Gain" and "loss"

(1)   The references to gain and loss in sections 2 to 4 are to be read in accordance with this section.

(2)   "Gain" and "loss"—

(a)   extend only to gain or loss in money or other property;

(b)   include any such gain or loss whether temporary or permanent;

and "property" means any property whether real or personal (including things in action and other intangible property).

(3)   "Gain" includes a gain by keeping what one has, as well as a gain by getting what one does not have.

(4)   "Loss" includes a loss by not getting what one might get, as well as a loss by parting with what one has.

6   **Possession etc. of articles for use in frauds**

(1)   A person is guilty of an offence if he has in his possession or under his control any article for use in the course of or in connection with any fraud.

(2)   A person guilty of an offence under this section is liable—

(a)   on summary conviction, to imprisonment for a term not exceeding 12 months or to a fine not exceeding the statutory maximum (or to both);

(b)   on conviction on indictment, to imprisonment for a term not exceeding 5 years or to a fine (or to both).

(3)   Subsection (2)(a) applies in relation to Northern Ireland as if the reference to 12 months were a reference to 6 months.

7   **Making or supplying articles for use in frauds**

(1)   A person is guilty of an offence if he makes, adapts, supplies or offers to supply any article—

(a)   knowing that it is designed or adapted for use in the course of or in connection with fraud, or

(b)   intending it to be used to commit, or assist in the commission of, fraud.

(2)   A person guilty of an offence under this section is liable—

(a)   on summary conviction, to imprisonment for a term not exceeding 12 months or to a fine not exceeding the statutory maximum (or to both);

(b)   on conviction on indictment, to imprisonment for a term not exceeding 10 years or to a fine (or to both).

(3)   Subsection (2)(a) applies in relation to Northern Ireland as if the reference to 12 months were a reference to 6 months.

8   **"Article"**

(1)   For the purposes of—

(a)   sections 6 and 7, and

(b)   the provisions listed in subsection (2), so far as they relate to articles for use in the course of or in connection with fraud,
"article" includes any program or data held in electronic form.

(2)   The provisions are—

(a)   section 1(7)(b) of the Police and Criminal Evidence Act 1984 (c. 60),

(b)   section 2(8)(b) of the Armed Forces Act 2001 (c. 19), and

(c)   Article 3(7)(b) of the Police and Criminal Evidence (Northern Ireland) Order 1989 (S.I. 1989/1341 (N.I. 12));

(meaning of "prohibited articles" for the purposes of stop and search powers).

9   **Participating in fraudulent business carried on by sole trader etc.**

(1)   A person is guilty of an offence if he is knowingly a party to the carrying on of a business to which this section applies.

(2)   This section applies to a business which is carried on—

(a)   by a person who is outside the reach of [section 993 of the Companies Act 2006](offence of fraudulent trading) , and

(b)   with intent to defraud creditors of any person or for any other fraudulent purpose.

(3)   The following are within the reach of [that section]—

(a)   a company [(as defined in section 1(1) of the Companies Act 2006)];

(b)   a person to whom that section applies (with or without adaptations or modifications) as if the person were a company;

(c)   a person exempted from the application of that section.

(4)   . . . .

(5)   "Fraudulent purpose" has the same meaning as in [that section].

(6)   A person guilty of an offence under this section is liable—

(a)   on summary conviction, to imprisonment for a term not exceeding 12 months or to a fine not exceeding the statutory maximum (or to both);

(b)   on conviction on indictment, to imprisonment for a term not exceeding 10 years or to a fine (or to both).

(7)   Subsection (6)(a) applies in relation to Northern Ireland as if the reference to 12 months were a reference to 6 months.

10   . . . .

OBTAINING SERVICES DISHONESTLY

11   **Obtaining services dishonestly**

(1)   A person is guilty of an offence under this section if he obtains services for himself or another—

(a)   by a dishonest act, and

(b)   in breach of subsection (2).

(2)   A person obtains services in breach of this subsection if—

(a)   they are made available on the basis that payment has been, is being or will be made for or in respect of them,

(b)   he obtains them without any payment having been made for or in respect of them or without payment having been made in full, and

(c)   when he obtains them, he knows—

(i) that they are being made available on the basis described in paragraph (a), or

(ii) that they might be,

but intends that payment will not be made, or will not be made in full.

(3) A person guilty of an offence under this section is liable—

(a) on summary conviction, to imprisonment for a term not exceeding 12 months or to a fine not exceeding the statutory maximum (or to both);

(b) on conviction on indictment, to imprisonment for a term not exceeding 5 years or to a fine (or to both).

(4) Subsection (3)(a) applies in relation to Northern Ireland as if the reference to 12 months were a reference to 6 months.

SUPPLEMENTARY

12 **Liability of company officers for offences by company**

(1) Subsection (2) applies if an offence under this Act is committed by a body corporate.

(2) If the offence is proved to have been committed with the consent or connivance of—

(a) a director, manager, secretary or other similar officer of the body corporate, or

(b) a person who was purporting to act in any such capacity,

he (as well as the body corporate) is guilty of the offence and liable to be proceeded against and punished accordingly.

(3) If the affairs of a body corporate are managed by its members, subsection (2) applies in relation to the acts and defaults of a member in connection with his functions of management as if he were a director of the body corporate.

Homicide Act 1957

1957 c. 11

PART I

AMENDMENTS OF LAW OF ENGLAND AND WALES AS TO FACT OF MURDER

1 **Abolition of "constructive malice".**

(1) Where a person kills another in the course or furtherance of some other

offence, the killing shall not amount to murder unless done with the same malice aforethought (express or implied) as is required for a killing to amount to murder when not done in the course or furtherance of another offence.

(2) For the purposes of the foregoing subsection, a killing done in the course or for the purpose of resisting an officer of justice, or of resisting or avoiding or preventing a lawful arrest, or of effecting or assisting an escape or rescue from legal custody, shall be treated as a killing in the course or furtherance of an offence.

2   **Persons suffering from diminished responsibility.**

[(1) A person ("D") who kills or is a party to the killing of another is not to be convicted of murder if D was suffering from an abnormality of mental functioning which—

(a) arose from a recognised medical condition,

(b) substantially impaired D's ability to do one or more of the things mentioned in subsection (1A), and

(c) provides an explanation for D's acts and omissions in doing or being a party to the killing.

(1A) Those things are

(a) to understand the nature of D's conduct;

(b) to form a rational judgment;

(c) to exercise self-control.

(1B) For the purposes of subsection (1)(c), an abnormality of mental functioning provides an explanation for D's conduct if it causes, or is a significant contributory factor in causing, D to carry out that conduct.]

(2) On a charge of murder, it shall be for the defence to prove that the person charged is by virtue of this section not liable to be convicted of murder.

(3) A person who but for this section would be liable, whether as principal or as accessory, to be convicted of murder shall be liable instead to be convicted of manslaughter.

(4) The fact that one party to a killing is by virtue of this section not liable to be convicted of murder shall not affect the question whether the killing amounted to murder in the case of any other party to it.

3   . . . .

4   **Suicide pacts.**

(1) It shall be manslaughter, and shall not be murder, for a person acting in pursuance of a suicide pact between him and another to kill the other or be a party to the other . . . being killed by a third person.

(2) Where it is shown that a person charged with the murder of another killed the other or was a party to his . . . being killed, it shall be for the defence

to prove that the person charged was acting in pursuance of a suicide pact between him and the other.

(3)   For the purposes of this section "suicide pact" means a common agreement between two or more persons having for its object the death of all of them, whether or not each is to take his own life, but nothing done by a person who enters into a suicide pact shall be treated as done by him in pursuance of the pact unless it is done while he has the settled intention of dying in pursuance of the pact.

Infanticide Act 1938

1938 c. 36

1   Offence of infanticide.

(1)   Where a woman by any wilful act or omission causes the death of her child being a child under the age of twelve months, but at the time of the act or omission the balance of her mind was disturbed by reason of her not having fully recovered from the effect of giving birth to the child or by reason of the effect of lactation consequent upon the birth of the child, then, [if] the circumstances were such that but for this Act the offence would have amounted to murder [or manslaughter], she shall be guilty of felony, to wit of infanticide, and may for such offence be dealt with and punished as if she had been guilty of the offence of manslaughter of the child.

(2)   Where upon the trial of a woman for the murder [or manslaughter] of her child, being a child under the age of twelve months, the jury are of opinion that she by any wilful act or omission caused its death, but that at the time of the act or omission the balance of her mind was disturbed by reason of her not having fully recovered from the effect of giving birth to the child or by reason of the effect of lactation consequent upon the birth of the child, then the jury may, [if] the circumstances were such that but for the provisions of this Act they might have returned a verdict of murder [or manslaughter], return in lieu thereof a verdict of infanticide.

(3)   Nothing in this Act shall affect the power of the jury upon an indictment for the murder of a child to return a verdict of manslaughter, or a verdict of guilty but insane, . . .

(4)   . . . .

Law Reform (Year and a Day Rule) Act 1996

1996 c. 19

Be it enacted by the Queen's most Excellent Majesty, by and with the advice and consent of the

Lords Spiritual and Temporal, and Commons, in this present Parliament assembled, and by the authority of the same, as follows:—

1 **Abolition of "year and a day rule".**

The rule known as the "year and a day rule" (that is, the rule that, for the purposes of offences involving death and of suicide, an act or omission is conclusively presumed not to have caused a person's death if more than a year and a day elapsed before he died) is abolished for all purposes.

2 **Restriction on institution of proceedings for a fatal offence.**

(1) Proceedings to which this section applies may only be instituted by or with the consent of the Attorney General.

(2) This section applies to proceedings against a person for a fatal offence if—

(a) the injury alleged to have caused the death was sustained more than three years before the death occurred, or

(b) the person has previously been convicted of an offence committed in circumstances alleged to be connected with the death.

(3) In subsection (2) "fatal offence" means—

(a) murder, manslaughter, infanticide or any other offence of which one of the elements is causing a person's death, . . .

[(b) an offence under section 2(1) of the Suicide Act 1961 (offence of encouraging or assisting suicide) in connection with the death of a person,] [or

(c) an offence under section 5 of the Domestic Violence, Crime and Victims Act 2004 [of causing or allowing the death of a child or vulnerable adult].]

(4) No provision that proceedings may be instituted only by or with the consent of the Director of Public Prosecutions shall apply to proceedings to which this section applies.

(5) In the application of this section to Northern Ireland—

(a) the reference in subsection (1) to the Attorney General is to the Attorney General for Northern Ireland, and

[(aa) the reference in subsection (3)(b) to section 2(1) of the Suicide Act 1961 is to be read as a reference to section 13(1) of the Criminal Justice Act (Northern Ireland) 1966, and]

(b) the reference in subsection (4) to the Director of Public Prosecutions is to the Director of Public Prosecutions for Northern Ireland.

3 **Short title, commencement and extent.**

(1) This Act may be cited as the Law Reform (Year and a Day Rule) Act 1996.

(2) Section 1 does not affect the continued application of the rule referred to in that section to a case where the act or omission (or the last of the acts or omissions) which caused the death occurred before the day on which this

Act is passed.

(3)   Section 2 does not come into force until the end of the period of two months beginning with the day on which this Act is passed; but that section applies to the institution of proceedings after the end of that period in any case where the death occurred during that period (as well as in any case where the death occurred after the end of that period).

(4)   This Act extends to England and Wales and Northern Ireland.

Misuse of Drugs Act 1971

1971 c. 38

CONTROLLED DRUGS AND THEIR CLASSIFICATION

2   **Controlled drugs and their classification for purposes of this Act.**

(1)   In this Act—

(a)   the expression "controlled drug" means any substance or product for the time being specified [—

(i)   in Part I, II or III of Schedule 2, or

(ii)   in a temporary class drug order as a drug subject to temporary control (but this is subject to section 2A(6));]

(b)   the expressions "Class A drug", "Class B drug" and "Class C drug" mean any of the substances and products for the time being specified respectively in Part I, Part II and Part III of that Schedule;

[(c)   the expression "temporary class drug" means any substance or product which is for the time being a controlled drug by virtue of a temporary class drug order;]

and the provisions of Part IV of that Schedule shall have effect with respect to the meanings of expressions used in that Schedule.

(2)   Her Majesty may by Order in Council make such amendments in Schedule 2 to this Act as may be requisite for the purpose of adding any substance or product to, or removing any substance or product from, any of Parts I to III of that Schedule, including amendments for securing that no substance or product is for the time being specified in a particular one of those Parts or for inserting any substance or product into any of those Parts in which no substance or product is for the time being specified.

(3)   An Order in Council under this section may amend Part IV of Schedule 2 to this Act, and may do so whether or not it amends any other Part of this Schedule.

(4)   An Order in Council under this section may be varied or revoked by a subsequent Order in Council thereunder.

(5)   No recommendation shall be made to Her Majesty in Council to make an Order under this section unless a draft of the Order has been laid before Parliament and approved by a resolution of each House of Parliament; and the Secretary of State shall not lay a draft of such an Order before Parliament except after consultation with or on the recommendation of the Advisory Council.

RESTRICTIONS RELATING TO CONTROLLED DRUGS ETC.

3   **Restriction of importation and exportation of controlled drugs.**

(1)   Subject to subsection (2) below—

(a)   the importation of a controlled drug; and

(b)   the exportation of a controlled drug,

are hereby prohibited.

(2)   Subsection (1) above does not apply—

(a)   to the importation or exportation of a controlled drug which is for the time being excepted from paragraph (a) or, as the case may be, paragraph (b) of subsection (1) above by regulations under section 7 of this Act [or by provision made in a temporary class drug order by virtue of section 7A]; or

(b)   to the importation or exportation of a controlled drug under and in accordance with the terms of a licence issued by the Secretary of State and in compliance with any conditions attached thereto.

4   **Restriction of production and supply of controlled drugs.**

(1)   Subject to any regulations under section 7 of this Act [, or any provision made in a temporary class drug order by virtue of section 7A] for the time being in force, it shall not be lawful for a person—

(a)   to produce a controlled drug; or

(b)   to supply or offer to supply a controlled drug to another.

(2)   Subject to section 28 of this Act, it is an offence for a person—

(a)   to produce a controlled drug in contravention of subsection (1) above; or

(b)   to be concerned in the production of such a drug in contravention of that subsection by another.

(3)   Subject to section 28 of this Act, it is an offence for a person—

(a)   to supply or offer to supply a controlled drug to another in contravention of subsection (1) above; or

(b)   to be concerned in the supplying of such a drug to another in contravention of that subsection; or

(c)   to be concerned in the making to another in contravention of that subsection of an offer to supply such a drug.

5 **Restriction of possession of controlled drugs.**

(1) Subject to any regulations under section 7 of this Act for the time being in force, it shall not be lawful for a person to have a controlled drug in his possession.

(2) Subject to section 28 of this Act and to subsection (4) below, it is an offence for a person to have a controlled drug in his possession in contravention of subsection (1) above.

[(2A) Subsections (1) and (2) do not apply in relation to a temporary class drug.]

(3) Subject to section 28 of this Act, it is an offence for a person to have a controlled drug in his possession, whether lawfully or not, with intent to supply it to another in contravention of section 4(1) of this Act.

(4) In any proceedings for an offence under subsection (2) above in which it is proved that the accused had a controlled drug in his possession, it shall be a defence for him to prove—

(a) that, knowing or suspecting it to be a controlled drug, he took possession of it for the purpose of preventing another from committing or continuing to commit an offence in connection with that drug and that as soon as possible after taking possession of it he took all such steps as were reasonably open to him to destroy the drug or to deliver it into the custody of a person lawfully entitled to take custody of it; or

(b) that, knowing or suspecting it to be a controlled drug, he took possession of it for the purpose of delivering it into the custody of a person lawfully entitled to take custody of it and that as soon as possible after taking possession of it he took all such steps as were reasonably open to him to deliver it into the custody of such a person.

(4A) . . . .

(4B) . . . .

(4C) . . . .

[(5) Subsection (4) above shall apply in the case of proceedings for an offence under section 19(1) of this Act consisting of an attempt to commit an offence under subsection (2) above as it applies in the case of proceedings for an offence under subsection (2), subject to the following modifications, that is to say—

(a) for the references to the accused having in his possession, and to his taking possession of, a controlled drug there shall be substituted respectively references to his attempting to get, and to his attempting to take, possession of such a drug; and

(b) in paragraphs (a) and (b) the words from "and that as soon as possible" onwards shall be omitted.]

(6) Nothing in subsection (4) [or (5)] above shall prejudice any defence which it

is open to a person charged with an offence under this section to raise apart from that subsection.

6   **Restriction of cultivation of cannabis plant.**

(1)   Subject to any regulations under section 7 of this Act for the time being in force, it shall not be lawful for a person to cultivate any plant of the genus-*Cannabis*.

(2)   Subject to section 28 of this Act, it is an offence to cultivate any such plant in contravention subsection (1) above.

MISCELLANEOUS OFFENCES INVOLVING CONTROLLED DRUGS ETC.

8   **Occupiers etc. of premises to be punishable for permitting certain activities to take place there.**
A person commits an offence if, being the occupier or concerned in the management of any premises, he knowingly permits or suffers any of the following activities to take place on those premises, that is to say—

(a)   producing or attempting to produce a controlled drug in contravention of section 4(1) of this Act;

(b)   supplying or attempting to supply a controlled drug to another in contravention of section 4(1) of this Act, or offering to supply a controlled drug to another in contravention of section 4(1);

(c)   preparing opium for smoking;

[(d)   administering or using a controlled drug which is unlawfully in any person's possession at or immediately before the time when it is administered or used.]

MISCELLANEOUS AND SUPPLEMENTARY PROVISIONS

28   **Proof of lack of knowledge etc. to be a defence in proceedings for certain offences.**

(1)   This section applies to offences under any of the following provisions of this Act, that is to say section 4(2) and (3), section 5(2) and (3), section 6(2) and section 9.

(2)   Subject to subsection (3) below, in any proceedings for an offence to which this section applies it shall be a defence for the accused to prove that he neither knew of nor suspected nor had reason to suspect the existence of some fact alleged by the prosecution which it is necessary for the prosecution to prove if he is to be convicted of the offence charged.

(3)   Where in any proceedings for an offence to which this section applies it is necessary, if the accused is to be convicted of the offence charged, for the prosecution to prove that some substance or product involved in the alleged offence was the controlled drug which the prosecution alleges it to have

been, and it is proved that the substance or product in question was that controlled drug, the accused—

(a)   shall not be acquitted of the offence charged by reason only of proving that he neither knew nor suspected nor had reason to suspect that the substance or product in question was the particular controlled drug alleged; but

(b)   shall be acquitted thereof—

    (i)   if he proves that he neither believed nor suspected nor had reason to suspect that the substance or product in question was a controlled drug; or

    (ii)   if he proves that he believed the substance or product in question to be a controlled drug, or a controlled drug of a description, such that, if it had in fact been that controlled drug or a controlled drug of that description, he would not at the material time have been committing any offence to which this section applies.

(4)   Nothing in this section shall prejudice any defence which it is open to a person charged with an offence to which this section applies to raise apart from this section

Offences Against the Person Act 1861

1861 c. 100

HOMICIDE

4   **Conspiring or soliciting to commit murder.**

. . . . whosoever shall solicit, encourage, persuade, or endeavour to persuade, or shall propose to any person, to murder any other person, whether he be a subject of Her Majesty or not, and whether he be within the Queen's dominions or not, shall be guilty of a misdemeanor, and being convicted thereof shall be liable. . . . . to [imprisonment for life]. . . . .

9   **Murder or manslaughter abroad.**

Where any murder or manslaughter shall be committed on land out of the United Kingdom, whether within the Queen's dominions or without, and whether the person killed were a subject of Her Majesty or not, every offence committed by any subject of Her Majesty in respect of any such case, whether the same shall amount to the offence of murder or of manslaughter, . . . , may be dealt with, inquired of, tried, determined, and punished . . . in England or Ireland . . . : Provided, that nothing herein contained shall prevent any person from being tried in any place out of England or Ireland for any murder or manslaughter committed out of England or

Ireland, in the same manner as such person might have been tried before the passing of this Act.

10   **Provision for the trial of murder and manslaughter where the death or cause of death only happens in England or Ireland.**

Where any person being [criminally] stricken, poisoned, or otherwise hurt upon the sea, or at any place out of England or Ireland, shall die of such stroke, poisoning, or hurt in England or Ireland, or, being [criminally] stricken, poisoned, or otherwise hurt in any place in England or Ireland, shall die of such stroke, poisoning, or hurt upon the sea, or at any place out of England or Ireland, every offence committed in respect of any such case, whether the same shall amount to the offence of murder or of manslaughter, . . . , may be dealt with, inquired of, tried, determined, and punished . . . in England or Ireland . . .

LETTERS THREATENING TO MURDER

[16   Threats to kill.

A person who without lawful excuse makes to another a threat, intending that that other would fear it would be carried out, to kill that other or a third person shall be guilty of an offence and liable on conviction on indictment to imprisonment for a term not exceeding ten years.]

ACTS CAUSING OR TENDING TO CAUSE
DANGER TO LIFE OR BODILY HARM

17   **Impeding a person endeavouring to save himself from shipwreck.**

Whosoever shall unlawfully and maliciously prevent or impede any person, being on board of or having quitted any ship or vessel which shall be in distress, or wrecked, stranded, or cast on shore, in his endeavour to save his life, or shall unlawfully and maliciously prevent or impede any person in his endeavour to save the life of any such person as in this section first aforesaid, shall be guilty of felony, and being convicted thereof shall be liable . . . to be kept in penal servitude for life . . .

18   **Shooting or attempting to shoot, or wounding with intent to do grievous bodily harm.**

Whosoever shall unlawfully and maliciously by any means whatsoever wound or cause any grievous bodily harm to any person, . . . with intent, . . . to do some . . . grievous bodily harm to any person, or with intent to resist or prevent the lawful apprehension or detainer of any person, shall be guilty of felony, and being convicted thereof shall be liable . . . to be kept in penal servitude for life . . .

20   **Inflicting bodily injury, with or without weapon.**

Whosoever shall unlawfully and maliciously wound or inflict any grievous bodily harm upon any other person, either with or without any weapon or instrument, shall be guilty of a misdemeanor, and being convicted thereof shall be liable . . . to be kept in penal servitude . . .

21 Attempting to choke, &c. in order to commit any indictable offence.

Whosoever shall, by any means whatsoever, attempt to choke, suffocate, or strangle any other person, or shall by any means calculated to choke, suffocate, or strangle, attempt to render any other person insensible, unconscious, or incapable of resistance, with intent in any of such cases thereby to enable himself or any other person to commit, or with intent in any of such cases thereby to assist any other person in committing, any indictable offence, shall be guilty of felony, and being convicted thereof shall be liable . . . to be kept in penal servitude for life . . .

22 Using chloroform, &c. to commit any indictable offence.

Whosoever shall unlawfully apply or administer to or cause to be taken by, or attempt to apply or administer to or attempt to cause to be administered to or taken by, any person, any chloroform, laudanum, or other stupefying or overpowering drug, matter, or thing, with intent in any of such cases thereby to enable himself or any other person to commit, or with intent in any of such cases thereby to assist any other person in committing, any indictable offence, shall be guilty of felony, and being convicted thereof shall be liable . . . to be kept in penal servitude for life . . .

23 Maliciously administering poison, &c. so as to endanger life or inflict grievous bodily harm.

Whosoever shall unlawfully and maliciously administer to or cause to be administered to or taken by any other person any poison or other destructive or noxious thing, so as thereby to endanger the life of such person, or so as thereby to inflict upon such person any grievous bodily harm, shall be guilty of felony, and being convicted thereof shall be liable . . . to be kept in penal servitude for any term not exceeding ten years . . .

24 Maliciously administering poison, &c. with intent to injure, aggrieve, or annoy any other person.

Whosoever shall unlawfully and maliciously administer to or cause to be administered to or taken by any other person any poison or other destructive or noxious thing, with intent to injure, aggrieve, or annoy such person, shall be guilty of a misdemeanor, and being convicted thereof shall be liable . . . to be kept in penal servitude . . .

26 Not providing apprentices or servants with food, &c. whereby life is endangered.

Whosoever, being legally liable, either as a master or mistress, to provide for any apprentice or servant necessary food, clothing, or lodging, shall wilfully and without lawful excuse refuse or neglect to provide the same, or shall unlawfully and maliciously do or cause to be done any bodily harm to any such apprentice or servant, so that the life of such apprentice or servant shall be endangered, or the health of such apprentice or servant shall have been or shall be likely to be permanently injured, shall be guilty of a misdemeanor, and being convicted thereof shall be liable . . . to be kept in penal servitude . . .

27 Exposing children whereby life is endangered.

Whosoever shall unlawfully abandon or expose any child, being under the age of two years, whereby the life of such child shall be endangered, or the health of such child shall have been or shall be likely to be permanently injured, shall be guilty of a misdemeanor, and being convicted thereof shall be liable . . . to be kept in penal servitude . . .

28 Causing bodily injury by gunpowder.

Whosoever shall unlawfully and maliciously, by the explosion of gunpowder or other explosive substance, burn, maim, disfigure, disable, or do any grievous bodily harm to any person, shall be guilty of felony, and being convicted thereof shall be liable, at the discretion of the court, to be kept in penal servitude for life . . . or to be imprisoned . . .

29 Causing gunpowder to explode, or sending to any person an explosive substance, or throwing corrosive fluid on a person, with intent to do grievous bodily harm.

Whosoever shall unlawfully and maliciously cause any gunpowder or other explosive substance to explode, or send or deliver to or cause to be taken or received by any person any explosive substance or any other dangerous or noxious thing, or put or lay at any place, or cast or throw at or upon or otherwise apply to any person, any corrosive fluid or any destructive or explosive substance, with intent in any of the cases aforesaid to burn, maim, disfigure, or disable any person, or to do some grievous bodily harm to any person, shall, whether any bodily injury be effected or not, be guilty of felony, and being convicted thereof shall be liable, at the discretion of the court, to be kept in penal servitude for life . . . or to be imprisoned . . .

30 Placing gunpowder near a building, with intent to do bodily injury to any person.

Whosoever shall unlawfully and maliciously place or throw in, into, upon, against, or near any building, ship, or vessel any gunpowder or other explosive substance, with intent to do any bodily injury to any person, shall, whether or not any explosion take place, and whether or not any bodily injury be effected, be guilty of felony, and being convicted thereof shall be liable, at the discretion of the court, to be kept in penal servitude for any term not exceeding fourteen years . . . or to be imprisoned . . .

31 Setting spring guns, &c., with intent to inflict grievous bodily harm.

Whosoever shall set or place, or cause to be set or placed, any spring gun, man trap, or other engine calculated to destroy human life or inflict grievous bodily harm, with the intent that the same or whereby the same may destroy or inflict grievous bodily harm upon a trespasser or other person coming in contact therewith, shall be guilty of a misdemeanor, and being convicted thereof shall be liable . . . to be kept in penal servitude . . . ; and whosoever shall knowingly and wilfully permit any such spring gun, man trap, or other engine which may have been set or placed in any place then being in or afterwards coming into his possession or occupation by some other person to continue so set or placed, shall be deemed to have set and placed such gun, trap, or engine with such intent as aforesaid: Provided, that nothing in this section contained shall extend to make it illegal to set or place any gin or trap such as may have been or may be usually set or placed with the intent of destroying vermin: Provided also, that nothing in this section shall be deemed to make it unlawful to set or place, or cause to be set or placed, or to be continued set or placed, from sunset to sunrise, any spring gun, man trap, or other engine which shall be set or placed, or caused or continued to be set or placed, in a dwelling house, for the protection thereof.

32   **Placing wood, &c., on a railway, with intent to endanger passengers.**

Whosoever shall unlawfully and maliciously put or throw upon or across any railway any wood, stone, or other matter or thing, or shall unlawfully and maliciously take up, remove, or displace any rail, sleeper, or other matter or thing belonging to any railway, or shall unlawfully and maliciously turn, move, or divert any points or other machinery belonging to any railway, or shall unlawfully and maliciously make or show, hide or remove, any signal or light upon or near to any railway, or shall unlawfully and maliciously do or cause to be done any other matter or thing, with intent, in any of the cases aforesaid, to endanger the safety of any person travelling or being upon such railway, shall be guilty of felony, and being convicted thereof shall be liable, at the discretion of the court, to be kept in penal servitude for life . . . or to be imprisoned . . .

33   **Casting stone, &c. upon a railway carriage, with intent to endanger the safety of any person therein.**
Whosoever shall unlawfully and maliciously throw, or cause to fall or strike, at, against, into, or upon any engine, tender, carriage, or truck used upon any railway, any wood, stone, or other matter or thing, with intent to injure or endanger the safety of any person being in or upon such engine, tender, carriage, or truck, or in or upon any other engine, tender, carriage, or truck of any train of which such first-mentioned engine, tender, carriage, or truck shall form part, shall be guilty of felony, and being convicted thereof shall be liable . . . to be kept in penal servitude for life . . .

34   **Doing or omitting anything to endanger passengers by railway.**

Whosoever, by any unlawful act, or by any wilful omission or neglect, shall endanger or cause to be endangered the safety of any person conveyed or being in or upon a railway, or shall aid or assist therein, shall be guilty of a misdemeanor, and being convicted thereof shall be liable, at the discretion of the court, to be imprisoned for any term not exceeding two years, . . .

35   **Drivers of carriages injuring persons by furious driving.**

Whosoever, having the charge of any carriage or vehicle, shall by wanton or furious driving or racing, or other wilful misconduct, or by wilful neglect, do or cause to be done any bodily harm to any person whatsoever, shall be guilty of a misdemeanor, and being convicted thereof shall be liable, at the discretion of the court, to be imprisoned for any term not exceeding two years, . . .

ASSAULTS

38   **Assault with intent to commit felony, or on peace officers, &c.**

Whosoever ... shall assault any person with intent to resist or prevent the lawful apprehension or detainer of himself or of any other person for any offence, shall be guilty of a misdemeanor, and being convicted thereof shall be liable, at the discretion of the court, to be imprisoned for any term not exceeding two years, ...

47   **Assault occasioning bodily harm.**

Whosoever shall be convicted upon an indictment of any assault occasioning actual bodily harm shall be liable ... to be kept in penal servitude ...; ......

CHILD-STEALING

[56   **Child-stealing.**

Whosoever shall unlawfully, either by force or fraud, lead or take away, or decoy or entice away or detain, any child under the age of fourteen years, with intent to deprive any parent, guardian, or other person having the lawful care or charge of such child of the possession of such child, or with intent to steal any article upon or about the person of such child, to whomsoever such article may belong, and whosoever shall, with any such intent, receive or harbour any such child, knowing the same to have been, by force or fraud, led, taken, decoyed, enticed away, or detained, as in this section before mentioned, shall be guilty of felony, and being convicted thereof shall be liable, at the discretion of the court, to be kept in penal servitude for any term not exceeding seven years ... or to be imprisoned .... Provided, that no person who shall have claimed any right to the possession of such child, or shall be the mother or shall have claimed to be the father of an illegitimate child, shall be liable to be prosecuted by virtue hereof on account of the getting possession of such child, or taking such child out of the possession of any person having the lawful charge thereof.]

BIGAMY

57   **Bigamy. Offence may be dealt with where offender shall be apprehended. Not to extend to second marriages, &c. herein stated.**

Whosoever, being married, shall marry any other person during the life of the former husband or wife, whether the second marriage shall have taken place in England or Ireland or elsewhere, shall be guilty of felony, and being convicted thereof shall be liable ... to be kept in penal servitude for any term not exceeding seven years ... : Provided, that nothing in this section contained shall extend to any second marriage contracted elsewhere than in England and Ireland by any other than a subject of Her Majesty, or to any person marrying a second time whose husband or wife shall have been continually absent from such person for the space of seven years then last past, and shall not have been known by such person to be living within that time, or shall extend to any person who, at the time of such second marriage, shall have been divorced from the bond of the first marriage, or to any person whose former marriage shall have been declared void by the sentence of any court of competent jurisdiction.

ATTEMPTS TO PROCURE ABORTION

58   **Administering drugs or using instruments to procure abortion.**

Every woman, being with child, who, with intent to procure her own miscarriage, shall unlawfully administer to herself any poison or other noxious thing, or shall unlawfully use any instrument or other means whatsoever with the like intent, and whosoever, with intent to procure the miscarriage of any woman, whether she be or be not with child, shall unlawfully administer to her or cause to be taken by her any poison or other noxious thing, or shall unlawfully use any instrument or other means whatsoever with the like intent, shall be guilty of felony, and being convicted thereof shall be liable . . . to be kept in penal servitude for life . . .

59   **Procuring drugs, &c. to cause abortion.**

Whosoever shall unlawfully supply or procure any poison or other noxious thing, or any instrument or thing whatsoever, knowing that the same is intended to be unlawfully used or employed with intent to procure the miscarriage of any woman, whether she be or be not with child, shall be guilty of a misdemeanor, and being convicted thereof shall be liable . . . to be kept in penal servitude . . .

CONCEALING THE BIRTH OF A CHILD

60   **Concealing the birth of a child.**

If any woman shall be delivered of a child, every person who shall, by any secret disposition of the dead body of the said child, whether such child died before, at, or after its birth, endeavour to conceal the birth thereof, shall be guilty of a misdemeanor, and being convicted thereof shall be liable, at the discretion of the court, to be imprisoned for any term not exceeding two years, . . .

MAKING GUNPOWDER TO COMMIT OFFENCES, AND SEARCHING FOR THE SAME

[64   **Making or having gunpowder, &c., with intent to commit any felony against this Act.**

Whosoever shall knowingly have in his possession, or make or manufacture, any gunpowder, explosive substance, or any dangerous or noxious thing, or any machine, engine, instrument, or thing, with intent by means thereof to commit, or for the purpose of enabling any other person to commit, any of the felonies in this Act mentioned shall be guilty of a misdemeanor, and being convicted thereof shall be liable, at the discretion of the court, to be imprisoned for any term not exceeding two years, . . .]

ASSAULTS

54, 55. . . . .

Protection from Harassment Act 1997

1997 c. 40

ENGLAND AND WALES

1   **Prohibition of harassment.**

(1)   A person must not pursue a course of conduct—

      (a)   which amounts to harassment of another, and

      (b)   which he knows or ought to know amounts to harassment of the other.

[(1A)   A person must not pursue a course of conduct —

      (a)   which involves harassment of two or more persons, and

      (b)   which he knows or ought to know involves harassment of those persons, and

      (c)   by which he intends to persuade any person (whether or not one of those mentioned above)—

          (i)   not to do something that he is entitled or required to do, or

          (ii)   to do something that he is not under any obligation to do.]

(2)   For the purposes of or [section 2A(2)(c)], the person whose course of conduct is in question ought to know that it amounts to [or involves] harassment of another if a reasonable person in possession of the same information would think the course of conduct amounted to [or involved] harassment of the other.

(3)   Subsection (1) [or (1A)] does not apply to a course of conduct if the person who pursued it shows—

      (a)   that it was pursued for the purpose of preventing or detecting crime,

      (b)   that it was pursued under any enactment or rule of law or to comply with any condition or requirement imposed by any person under any enactment, or

      (c)   that in the particular circumstances the pursuit of the course of conduct was reasonable.

2   **Offence of harassment.**

(1)   A person who pursues a course of conduct in breach of [section 1(1) or (1A)] is guilty of an offence.

(2)   A person guilty of an offence under this section is liable on summary conviction to imprisonment for a term not exceeding six months, or a fine not exceeding level 5 on the standard scale, or both.

(3)   . . . .

[2A   **Offence of stalking**

(1)   A person is guilty of an offence if—

(a)   the person pursues a course of conduct in breach of section 1(1), and

(b)   the course of conduct amounts to stalking.

(2)   For the purposes of subsection (1)(b) (and section 4A(1)(a)) a person's course of conduct amounts to stalking of another person if—

(a)   it amounts to harassment of that person,

(b)   the acts or omissions involved are ones associated with stalking, and

(c)   the person whose course of conduct it is knows or ought to know that the course of conduct amounts to harassment of the other person.

(3)   The following are examples of acts or omissions which, in particular circumstances, are ones associated with stalking—

(a)   following a person,

(b)   contacting, or attempting to contact, a person by any means,

(c)   publishing any statement or other material—

(i)   relating or purporting to relate to a person, or

(ii)   purporting to originate from a person,

(d)   monitoring the use by a person of the internet, email or any other form of electronic communication,

(e)   loitering in any place (whether public or private),

(f)   interfering with any property in the possession of a person,

(g)   watching or spying on a person.

(4)   A person guilty of an offence under this section is liable on summary conviction to imprisonment for a term not exceeding 51 weeks, or a fine not exceeding level 5 on the standard scale, or both.

(5)   In relation to an offence committed before the commencement of section 281(5) of the Criminal Justice Act 2003, the reference in subsection (4) to 51 weeks is to be read as a reference to six months.

(6)   This section is without prejudice to the generality of section 2.]

[2B   **Power of entry in relation to offence of stalking**

(1)   A justice of the peace may, on an application by a constable, issue a warrant authorising a constable to enter and search premises if the justice of the peace is satisfied that there are reasonable grounds for believing that—

(a)   an offence under section 2A has been, or is being, committed,

(b)   there is material on the premises which is likely to be of substantial value (whether by itself or together with other material) to the investigation of the offence,

(c)   the material—

    (i)   is likely to be admissible in evidence at a trial for the offence, and

    (ii)   does not consist of, or include, items subject to legal privilege, excluded material or special procedure material (within the meanings given by sections 10, 11 and 14 of the Police and Criminal Evidence Act 1984), and

(d)   either—

    (i)   entry to the premises will not be granted unless a warrant is produced, or

    (ii)   the purpose of a search may be frustrated or seriously prejudiced unless a constable arriving at the premises can secure immediate entry to them.

(2)   A constable may seize and retain anything for which a search has been authorised under subsection (1).

(3)   A constable may use reasonable force, if necessary, in the exercise of any power conferred by virtue of this section.

(4)   In this section "premises" has the same meaning as in section 23 of the Police and Criminal Evidence Act 1984.]

3   **Civil remedy.**

(1)   An actual or apprehended breach of [section 1(1)] may be the subject of a claim in civil proceedings by the person who is or may be the victim of the course of conduct in question.

(2)   On such a claim, damages may be awarded for (among other things) any anxiety caused by the harassment and any financial loss resulting from the harassment.

(3)   Where—

(a)   in such proceedings the High Court or a county court grants an injunction for the purpose of restraining the defendant from pursuing any conduct which amounts to harassment, and

(b)   the plaintiff considers that the defendant has done anything which he is prohibited from doing by the injunction,

the plaintiff may apply for the issue of a warrant for the arrest of the defendant.

(4)   An application under subsection (3) may be made—

(a)   where the injunction was granted by the High Court, to a judge of that court, and

(b)   where the injunction was granted by a county court, to a judge or district judge of that or any other county court.

(5)   The judge or district judge to whom an application under subsection (3) is made may only issue a warrant if—

    (a)   the application is substantiated on oath, and

    (b)   the judge or district judge has reasonable grounds for believing that the defendant has done anything which he is prohibited from doing by the injunction.

(6)   Where—

    (a)   the High Court or a county court grants an injunction for the purpose mentioned in subsection (3)(a), and

    (b)   without reasonable excuse the defendant does anything which he is prohibited from doing by the injunction,

he is guilty of an offence.

(7)   Where a person is convicted of an offence under subsection (6) in respect of any conduct, that conduct is not punishable as a contempt of court.

(8)   A person cannot be convicted of an offence under subsection (6) in respect of any conduct which has been punished as a contempt of court.

(9)   A person guilty of an offence under subsection (6) is liable—

    (a)   on conviction on indictment, to imprisonment for a term not exceeding five years, or a fine, or both, or

    (b)   on summary conviction, to imprisonment for a term not exceeding six months, or a fine not exceeding the statutory maximum, or both.

[3A   **Injunctions to protect persons from harassment within section 1(1A)**

(1)   This section applies where there is an actual or apprehended breach of section 1(1A) by any person ("the relevant person").

(2)   In such a case—

    (a)   any person who is or may be a victim of the course of conduct in question, or

    (b)   any person who is or may be a person falling within section 1(1A) (c),

may apply to the High Court or a county court for an injunction restraining the relevant person from pursuing any conduct which amounts to harassment in relation to any person or persons mentioned or described in the injunction.

(3)   Section 3(3) to (9) apply in relation to an injunction granted under subsection (2) above as they apply in relation to an injunction granted as mentioned in section 3(3)(a).]

4   **Putting people in fear of violence.**

(1)   A person whose course of conduct causes another to fear, on at least two

occasions, that violence will be used against him is guilty of an offence if he knows or ought to know that his course of conduct will cause the other so to fear on each of those occasions.

(2)   For the purposes of this section, the person whose course of conduct is in question ought to know that it will cause another to fear that violence will be used against him on any occasion if a reasonable person in possession of the same information would think the course of conduct would cause the other so to fear on that occasion.

(3)   It is a defence for a person charged with an offence under this section to show that—

(a)   his course of conduct was pursued for the purpose of preventing or detecting crime,

(b)   his course of conduct was pursued under any enactment or rule of law or to comply with any condition or requirement imposed by any person under any enactment, or

(c)   the pursuit of his course of conduct was reasonable for the protection of himself or another or for the protection of his or another's property.

(4)   A person guilty of an offence under this section is liable—

(a)   on conviction on indictment, to imprisonment for a term not exceeding five years, or a fine, or both, or

(b)   on summary conviction, to imprisonment for a term not exceeding six months, or a fine not exceeding the statutory maximum, or both.

(5)   If on the trial on indictment of a person charged with an offence under this section the jury find him not guilty of the offence charged, they may find him guilty of an offence under section 2 [or 2A].

(6)   The Crown Court has the same powers and duties in relation to a person who is by virtue of subsection (5) convicted before it of an offence under section 2 [or 2A] as a magistrates' court would have on convicting him of the offence.

[4A   **Stalking involving fear of violence or serious alarm or distress**

(1)   A person ("A") whose course of conduct—

(a)   amounts to stalking, and

(b)   either—

(i)   causes another ("B") to fear, on at least two occasions, that violence will be used against B, or

(ii)   causes B serious alarm or distress which has a substantial adverse effect on B's usual day-to-day activities,

is guilty of an offence if A knows or ought to know that A's course of conduct will cause B so to fear on each of those occasions or (as the case may be) will cause such alarm or distress.

(2)   For the purposes of this section A ought to know that A's course of conduct will cause B to fear that violence will be used against B on any occasion if a reasonable person in possession of the same information would think the course of conduct would cause B so to fear on that occasion.

(3)   For the purposes of this section A ought to know that A's course of conduct will cause B serious alarm or distress which has a substantial adverse effect on B's usual day-to-day activities if a reasonable person in possession of the same information would think the course of conduct would cause B such alarm or distress.

(4)   It is a defence for A to show that—

(a)   A's course of conduct was pursued for the purpose of preventing or detecting crime,

(b)   A's course of conduct was pursued under any enactment or rule of law or to comply with any condition or requirement imposed by any person under any enactment, or

(c)   the pursuit of A's course of conduct was reasonable for the protection of A or another or for the protection of A's or another's property.

(5)   A person guilty of an offence under this section is liable—

(a)   on conviction on indictment, to imprisonment for a term not exceeding five years, or a fine, or both, or

(b)   on summary conviction, to imprisonment for a term not exceeding twelve months, or a fine not exceeding the statutory maximum, or both.

(6)   In relation to an offence committed before the commencement of section 154(1) of the Criminal Justice Act 2003, the reference in subsection (5)(b) to twelve months is to be read as a reference to six months.

(7)   If on the trial on indictment of a person charged with an offence under this section the jury find the person not guilty of the offence charged, they may find the person guilty of an offence under section 2 or 2A.

(8)   The Crown Court has the same powers and duties in relation to a person who is by virtue of subsection (7) convicted before it of an offence under section 2 or 2A as a magistrates' court would have on convicting the person of the offence.

(9)   This section is without prejudice to the generality of section 4.]

5   Restraining orders [on conviction].

(1)   A court sentencing or otherwise dealing with a person ("the defendant") convicted of an offence . . . may (as well as sentencing him or dealing with him in any other way) make an order under this section.

(2)   The order may, for the purpose of protecting the victim [or victims] of the offence, or any other person mentioned in the order, from . . . conduct which

—

(a)   amounts to harassment, or

(b)   will cause a fear of violence,

prohibit the defendant from doing anything described in the order.

(3)   The order may have effect for a specified period or until further order.

[(3A) In proceedings under this section both the prosecution and the defence may lead, as further evidence, any evidence that would be admissible in proceedings for an injunction under section 3.]

(4)   The prosecutor, the defendant or any other person mentioned in the order may apply to the court which made the order for it to be varied or discharged by a further order.

[(4A) Any person mentioned in the order is entitled to be heard on the hearing of an application under subsection (4).]

(5)   If without reasonable excuse the defendant does anything which he is prohibited from doing by an order under this section, he is guilty of an offence.

(6)   A person guilty of an offence under this section is liable—

(a)   on conviction on indictment, to imprisonment for a term not exceeding five years, or a fine, or both, or

(b)   on summary conviction, to imprisonment for a term not exceeding six months, or a fine not exceeding the statutory maximum, or both.

[(7)   A court dealing with a person for an offence under this section may vary or discharge the order in question by a further order.]

[5A   **Restraining orders on acquittal**

(1)   A court before which a person ("the defendant") is acquitted of an offence may, if it considers it necessary to do so to protect a person from harassment by the defendant, make an order prohibiting the defendant from doing anything described in the order.

(2)   Subsections (3) to (7) of section 5 apply to an order under this section as they apply to an order under that one.

(3)   Where the Court of Appeal allow an appeal against conviction they may remit the case to the Crown Court to consider whether to proceed under this section.

(4)   Where—

(a)   the Crown Court allows an appeal against conviction, or

(b)   a case is remitted to the Crown Court under subsection (3),

the reference in subsection (1) to a court before which a person is acquitted of an offence is to be read as referring to that court.

(5)   A person made subject to an order under this section has the same right of appeal against the order as if—

(a)   he had been convicted of the offence in question before the court which made the order, and

    (b)   the order had been made under section 5.]

6   **Limitation.**

In section 11 of the Limitation Act 1980 (special time limit for actions in respect of personal injuries), after subsection (1) there is inserted—

"(1A)   This section does not apply to any action brought for damages under section 3 of the Protection from Harassment Act 1997."

7   **Interpretation of this group of sections.**

    (1)   This section applies for the interpretation of [sections 1 to 5A].

    (2)   References to harassing a person include alarming the person or causing the person distress.

    [(3)   A "course of conduct" must involve—

        (a)   in the case of conduct in relation to a single person (see section 1(1)), conduct on at least two occasions in relation to that person, or

        (b)   in the case of conduct in relation to two or more persons (see section 1(1A)), conduct on at least one occasion in relation to each of those persons.]

    [(3A)   A person's conduct on any occasion shall be taken, if aided, abetted, counselled or procured by another—

        (a)   to be conduct on that occasion of the other (as well as conduct of the person whose conduct it is); and

        (b)   to be conduct in relation to which the other's knowledge and purpose, and what he ought to have known, are the same as they were in relation to what was contemplated or reasonably foreseeable at the time of the aiding, abetting, counselling or procuring.]

    (4)   "Conduct" includes speech.

    [(5)   References to a person, in the context of the harassment of a person, are references to a person who is an individual.]

Road Traffic Act 1988

1988 c. 52

PART I
PRINCIPAL ROAD SAFETY PROVISIONS

DRIVING OFFENCES

[1   **Causing death by dangerous driving.**

A person who causes the death of another person by driving a mechanically propelled vehicle dangerously on a road or other public place is guilty of an offence.]

[2   Dangerous driving.

A person who drives a mechanically propelled vehicle dangerously on a road or other public place is guilty of an offence.]

[2A   Meaning of dangerous driving.

(1)   For the purposes of sections 1 and 2 above a person is to be regarded as driving dangerously if (and, subject to subsection (2) below, only if)—

(a)   the way he drives falls far below what would be expected of a competent and careful driver, and

(b)   it would be obvious to a competent and careful driver that driving in that way would be dangerous.

(2)   A person is also to be regarded as driving dangerously for the purposes of sections 1 and 2 above if it would be obvious to a competent and careful driver that driving the vehicle in its current state would be dangerous.

(3)   In subsections (1) and (2) above "dangerous" refers to danger either of injury to any person or of serious damage to property; and in determining for the purposes of those subsections what would be expected of, or obvious to, a competent and careful driver in a particular case, regard shall be had not only to the circumstances of which he could be expected to be aware but also to any circumstances shown to have been within the knowledge of the accused.

(4)   In determining for the purposes of subsection (2) above the state of a vehicle, regard may be had to anything attached to or carried on or in it and to the manner in which it is attached or carried.]

[2B   Causing death by careless, or inconsiderate, driving

A person who causes the death of another person by driving a mechanically propelled vehicle on a road or other public place without due care and attention, or without reasonable consideration for other persons using the road or place, is guilty of an offence.]

[3   Careless, and inconsiderate, driving.

If a person drives a mechanically propelled vehicle on a road or other public place without due care and attention, or without reasonable consideration for other persons using the road or place, he is guilty of an offence.]

[3ZA   Meaning of careless, or inconsiderate, driving

(1)   This section has effect for the purposes of sections 2B and 3 above and section 3A below.

(2)   A person is to be regarded as driving without due care and attention if (and only if) the way he drives falls below what would be expected of a competent and careful driver.

(3)   In determining for the purposes of subsection (2) above what would be expected of a careful and competent driver in a particular case, regard shall be had not only to the circumstances of which he could be expected to be aware but also to any circumstances shown to have been within the knowledge of the accused.

(4)   A person is to be regarded as driving without reasonable consideration for other persons only if those persons are inconvenienced by his driving.]

[3ZB   **Causing death by driving: unlicensed, disqualified or uninsured drivers**

A person is guilty of an offence under this section if he causes the death of another person by driving a motor vehicle on a road and, at the time when he is driving, the circumstances are such that he is committing an offence under—

(a)   section 87(1) of this Act (driving otherwise than in accordance with a licence),

(b)   section 103(1)(b) of this Act (driving while disqualified), or

(c)   section 143 of this Act (using motor vehicle while uninsured or unsecured against third party risks).]

[3A   **Causing death by careless driving when under influence of drink or drugs.**

(1)   If a person causes the death of another person by driving a mechanically propelled vehicle on a road or other public place without due care and attention, or without reasonable consideration for other persons using the road or place, and—

(a)   he is, at the time when he is driving, unfit to drive through drink or drugs, or

(b)   he has consumed so much alcohol that the proportion of it in his breath, blood or urine at that time exceeds the prescribed limit, or

(c)   he is, within 18 hours after that time, required to provide a specimen in pursuance of section 7 of this Act, but without reasonable excuse fails to provide it, [or

(d)   he is required by a constable to give his permission for a laboratory test of a specimen of blood taken from him under section 7A of this Act, but without reasonable excuse fails to do so,]

he is guilty of an offence.

(2)   For the purposes of this section a person shall be taken to be unfit to drive at any time when his ability to drive properly is impaired.

(3)   Subsection (1)(b) [, (c) and (d)] above shall not apply in relation to a person driving a mechanically propelled vehicle other than a motor vehicle.]

MOTOR VEHICLES: DRINK AND DRUGS

4   **Driving, or being in charge, when under influence of drink or drugs.**

(1)   A person who, when driving or attempting to drive a [mechanically

propelled vehicle] on a road or other public place, is unfit to drive through drink or drugs is guilty of an offence.

(2)   Without prejudice to subsection (1) above, a person who, when in charge of a [mechanically propelled vehicle] which is on a road or other public place, is unfit to drive through drink or drugs is guilty of an offence.

(3)   For the purposes of subsection (2) above, a person shall be deemed not to have been in charge of a [mechanically propelled vehicle] if he proves that at the material time the circumstances were such that there was no likelihood of his driving it so long as he remained unfit to drive through drink or drugs.

(4)   The court may, in determining whether there was such a likelihood as is mentioned in subsection (3) above, disregard any injury to him and any damage to the vehicle.

(5)   For the purposes of this section, a person shall be taken to be unfit to drive if his ability to drive properly is for the time being impaired.

(6)   [...]

(7)   [...]

(8)   . . . .

5   **Driving or being in charge of a motor vehicle with alcohol concentration above prescribed limit.**

(1)   If a person—

(a)   drives or attempts to drive a motor vehicle on a road or other public place, or

(b)   is in charge of a motor vehicle on a road or other public place,

after consuming so much alcohol that the proportion of it in his breath, blood or urine exceeds the prescribed limit he is guilty of an offence.

(2)   It is a defence for a person charged with an offence under subsection (1)(b) above to prove that at the time he is alleged to have committed the offence the circumstances were such that there was no likelihood of his driving the vehicle whilst the proportion of alcohol in his breath, blood or urine remained likely to exceed the prescribed limit.

(3)   The court may, in determining whether there was such a likelihood as is mentioned in subsection (2) above, disregard any injury to him and any damage to the vehicle.

PART III
LICENSING OF DRIVERS OF VEHICLES

[EFFECTS OF DISQUALIFICATION]

[103   **Obtaining licence, or driving, while disqualified.**

(1)   A person is guilty of an offence if, while disqualified for holding or obtaining

a licence, he—

(a)   obtains a licence, or

(b)   drives a motor vehicle on a road.

(2)   A licence obtained by a person who is disqualified is of no effect (or, where the disqualification relates only to vehicles of a particular class, is of no effect in relation to vehicles of that class).

(3)   . . . .

(4)   [Subsection (1) above does] not apply in relation to disqualification by virtue of section 101 of this Act.

(5)   [Subsection (1)(b) above does] not apply in relation to disqualification by virtue of section 102 of this Act.

(6)   In the application of [subsection (1)] above to a person whose disqualification is limited to the driving of motor vehicles of a particular class by virtue of—

(a)   section 102 [117 or 117A] of this Act, or

(b)   subsection (9) of section 36 of the Road Traffic Offenders Act 1988 (disqualification until test is passed),

the references to disqualification for holding or obtaining a licence and driving motor vehicles are references to disqualification for holding or obtaining a licence to drive and driving motor vehicles of that class.]

PART VI
THIRD-PARTY LIABILITIES

COMPULSORY INSURANCE OR
SECURITY AGAINST THIRD-PARTY RISKS

143   Users of motor vehicles to be insured or secured against third-party risks.

(1)   Subject to the provisions of this Part of this Act—

(a)   a person must not use a motor vehicle on a road [or other public place] unless there is in force in relation to the use of the vehicle by that person such a policy of insurance or such a security in respect of third party risks as complies with the requirements of this Part of this Act, and

(b)   a person must not cause or permit any other person to use a motor vehicle on a road [or other public place] unless there is in force in relation to the use of the vehicle by that other person such a policy of insurance or such a security in respect of third party risks as complies with the requirements of this Part of this Act.

(2)   If a person acts in contravention of subsection (1) above he is guilty of an offence.

(3)   A person charged with using a motor vehicle in contravention of this section shall not be convicted if he proves—

    (a)   that the vehicle did not belong to him and was not in his possession under a contract of hiring or of loan,

    (b)   that he was using the vehicle in the course of his employment, and

    (c)   that he neither knew nor had reason to believe that there was not in force in relation to the vehicle such a policy of insurance or security as is mentioned in subsection (1) above.

(4)   This Part of this Act does not apply to invalid carriages.

PART VII
MISCELLANEOUS AND GENERAL

DUTIES IN CASE OF ACCIDENT

170   Duty of driver to stop, report accident and give information or documents.

(1)   This section applies in a case where, owing to the presence of a [mechanically propelled vehicle] on a road [or other public place], an accident occurs by which—

    (a)   personal injury is caused to a person other than the driver of that [mechanically propelled vehicle], or

    (b)   damage is caused—

        (i)   to a vehicle other than that [mechanically propelled vehicle] or a trailer drawn by that [mechanically propelled vehicle], or

        (ii)   to an animal other than an animal in or on that [mechanically propelled vehicle] or a trailer drawn by that [mechanically propelled vehicle], or

        (iii)   to any other property constructed on, fixed to, growing in or otherwise forming part of the land on which the road [or place] in question is situated or land adjacent to such land.

(2)   The driver of the [mechanically propelled vehicle] must stop and, if required to do so by any person having reasonable grounds for so requiring, give his name and address and also the name and address of the owner and the identification marks of the vehicle.

(3)   If for any reason the driver of the [mechanically propelled vehicle] does not give his name and address under subsection (2) above, he must report the accident.

(4)   A person who fails to comply with subsection (2) or (3) above is guilty of an offence.

(5)   If, in a case where this section applies by virtue of subsection (1)(a) above, the driver of [a motor vehicle] does not at the time of the accident produce

such a certificate of insurance or security, or other evidence, as is mentioned in section 165(2)(a) of this Act—

(a)   to a constable, or

(b)   to some person who, having reasonable grounds for so doing, has required him to produce it,

the driver must report the accident and produce such a certificate or other evidence.

This subsection does not apply to the driver of an invalid carriage.

(6)   To comply with a duty under this section to report an accident or to produce such a certificate of insurance or security, or other evidence, as is mentioned in section 165(2)(a) of this Act, the driver—

(a)   must do so at a police station or to a constable, and

(b)   must do so as soon as is reasonably practicable and, in any case, within twenty-four hours of the occurrence of the accident.

(7)   A person who fails to comply with a duty under subsection (5) above is guilty of an offence, but he shall not be convicted by reason only of a failure to produce a certificate or other evidence if, within [seven] days after the occurrence of the accident, the certificate or other evidence is produced at a police station that was specified by him at the time when the accident was reported.

(8)   In this section "animal" means horse, cattle, ass, mule, sheep, pig, goat or dog.

PART VII
MISCELLANEOUS AND GENERAL

OTHER DUTIES TO GIVE INFORMATION OR DOCUMENTS

171   Duty of owner of motor vehicle to give information for verifying compliance with requirement of compulsory insurance or security.

(1)   For the purpose of determining whether a motor vehicle was or was not being driven in contravention of section 143 of this Act on any occasion when the driver was required under section 165(1) or 170 of this Act to produce such a certificate of insurance or security, or other evidence, as is mentioned in section 165(2)(a) of this Act, the owner of the vehicle must give such information as he may be required, by or on behalf of a chief officer of police, to give.

(2)   A person who fails to comply with the requirement of subsection (1) above is guilty of an offence.

(3)   In this section "owner", in relation to a vehicle which is the subject of a hiring agreement, includes each party to the agreement.

[172   Duty to give information as to identity of driver etc in certain circumstances.

(1)　　This section applies—

    (a)　　to any offence under the preceding provisions of this Act except—

        (i)　　an offence under Part V, or

        (ii)　　an offence under section 13, 16, 51(2), 61(4), 67(9), 68(4), 96 or 120,

    and to an offence under section 178 of this Act,

    (b)　　to any offence under sections 25, 26 or 27 of the Road Traffic Offenders Act 1988,

    (c)　　to any offence against any other enactment relating to the use of vehicles on roads, . . . and

    (d)　　to manslaughter, or in Scotland culpable homicide, by the driver of a motor vehicle.

(2)　　Where the driver of a vehicle is alleged to be guilty of an offence to which this section applies—

    (a)　　the person keeping the vehicle shall give such information as to the identity of the driver as he may be required to give by or on behalf of a chief officer of police, and

    (b)　　any other person shall if required as stated above give any information which it is in his power to give and may lead to identification of the driver.

(3)　　Subject to the following provisions, a person who fails to comply with a requirement under subsection (2) above shall be guilty of an offence.

(4)　　A person shall not be guilty of an offence by virtue of paragraph (a) of subsection (2) above if he shows that he did not know and could not with reasonable diligence have ascertained who the driver of the vehicle was.

(5)　　Where a body corporate is guilty of an offence under this section and the offence is proved to have been committed with the consent or connivance of, or to be attributable to neglect on the part of, a director, manager, secretary or other similar officer of the body corporate, or a person who was purporting to act in any such capacity, he, as well as the body corporate, is guilty of that offence and liable to be proceeded against and punished accordingly.

(6)　　Where the alleged offender is a body corporate, or in Scotland a partnership or an unincorporated association, or the proceedings are brought against him by virtue of subsection (5) above or subsection (11) below, subsection (4) above shall not apply unless, in addition to the matters there mentioned, the alleged offender shows that no record was kept of the persons who drove the vehicle and that the failure to keep a record was reasonable.

(7)　　A requirement under subsection (2) may be made by written notice served by post; and where it is so made—

    (a)　　it shall have effect as a requirement to give the information within the period of 28 days beginning with the day on which the notice is served, and

(b)   the person on whom the notice is served shall not be guilty of an offence under this section if he shows either that he gave the information as soon as reasonably practicable after the end of that period or that it has not been reasonably practicable for him to give it.

(8)   Where the person on whom a notice under subsection (7) above is to be served is a body corporate, the notice is duly served if it is served on the secretary or clerk of that body.

(9)   For the purposes of section 7 of the Interpretation Act 1978 as it applies for the purposes of this section the proper address of any person in relation to the service on him of a notice under subsection (7) above is—

(a)   in the case of the secretary or clerk of a body corporate, that of the registered or principal office of that body or (if the body corporate is the registered keeper of the vehicle concerned) the registered address, and

(b)   in any other case, his last known address at the time of service.

(10)   In this section—

"registered address", in relation to the registered keeper of a vehicle, means the address recorded in the record kept under [the Vehicles Excise and Registration Act 1994] with respect to that vehicle as being that person's address, and

"registered keeper", in relation to a vehicle, means the person in whose name the vehicle is registered under that Act;

and references to the driver of a vehicle include references to the rider of a cycle.

(11)   Where, in Scotland, an offence under this section is committed by a partnership or by an unincorporated association other than a partnership and is proved to have been committed with the consent or connivance or in consequence of the negligence of a partner in the partnership or, as the case may be, a person concerned in the management or control of the association, he (as well as the partnership or association) shall be guilty of the offence.]

PART II
CONSTRUCTION AND USE OF VEHICLES AND EQUIPMENT

TESTS OF CERTAIN CLASSES OF GOODS VEHICLES

50   **Appeals against determinations.**

(1)   Any person aggrieved by a determination made on an examination under regulations under section 49 of this Act by the person in charge of the examination may appeal to [the Secretary of State].

(2) . . . .

(3) . . . .

(4) On the appeal the Secretary of State must cause the vehicle to be re-examined by an officer appointed by him for the purpose and must make such determination on the basis of the re-examination as he thinks fit.

(5) Regulations under section 49 of this Act may make the like provision in relation to a determination on an appeal under this section as they make in relation to a determination on an examination under the regulations.

Sexual Offences Act 2003

2003 c. 42

PART 1
SEXUAL OFFENCES

RAPE

1   **Rape**

(1) A person (A) commits an offence if—

(a) he intentionally penetrates the vagina, anus or mouth of another person (B) with his penis,

(b) B does not consent to the penetration, and

(c) A does not reasonably believe that B consents.

(2) Whether a belief is reasonable is to be determined having regard to all the circumstances, including any steps A has taken to ascertain whether B consents.

(3) Sections 75 and 76 apply to an offence under this section.

(4) A person guilty of an offence under this section is liable, on conviction on indictment, to imprisonment for life.

ASSAULT

2   **Assault by penetration**

(1) A person (A) commits an offence if—

(a) he intentionally penetrates the vagina or anus of another person (B) with a part of his body or anything else,

(b) the penetration is sexual,

(c) B does not consent to the penetration, and

(d) A does not reasonably believe that B consents.

(2)   Whether a belief is reasonable is to be determined having regard to all the circumstances, including any steps A has taken to ascertain whether B consents.

(3)   Sections 75 and 76 apply to an offence under this section.

(4)   A person guilty of an offence under this section is liable, on conviction on indictment, to imprisonment for life.

3   **Sexual assault**

(1)   A person (A) commits an offence if—

(a)   he intentionally touches another person (B),

(b)   the touching is sexual,

(c)   B does not consent to the touching, and

(d)   A does not reasonably believe that B consents.

(2)   Whether a belief is reasonable is to be determined having regard to all the circumstances, including any steps A has taken to ascertain whether B consents.

(3)   Sections 75 and 76 apply to an offence under this section.

(4)   A person guilty of an offence under this section is liable—

(a)   on summary conviction, to imprisonment for a term not exceeding 6 months or a fine not exceeding the statutory maximum or both;

(b)   on conviction on indictment, to imprisonment for a term not exceeding 10 years.

CAUSING SEXUAL ACTIVITY WITHOUT CONSENT

4   **Causing a person to engage in sexual activity without consent**

(1)   A person (A) commits an offence if—

(a)   he intentionally causes another person (B) to engage in an activity,

(b)   the activity is sexual,

(c)   B does not consent to engaging in the activity, and

(d)   A does not reasonably believe that B consents.

(2)   Whether a belief is reasonable is to be determined having regard to all the circumstances, including any steps A has taken to ascertain whether B consents.

(3)   Sections 75 and 76 apply to an offence under this section.

(4)   A person guilty of an offence under this section, if the activity caused involved—

(a)   penetration of B's anus or vagina,

(b)   penetration of B's mouth with a person's penis,

(c)   penetration of a person's anus or vagina with a part of B's body or by B with anything else, or

(d) penetration of a person's mouth with B's penis,

is liable, on conviction on indictment, to imprisonment for life.

(5) Unless subsection (4) applies, a person guilty of an offence under this section is liable—

(a) on summary conviction, to imprisonment for a term not exceeding 6 months or to a fine not exceeding the statutory maximum or both;

(b) on conviction on indictment, to imprisonment for a term not exceeding 10 years.

RAPE AND OTHER OFFENCES AGAINST CHILDREN UNDER 13

5 Rape of a child under 13

(1) A person commits an offence if—

(a) he intentionally penetrates the vagina, anus or mouth of another person with his penis, and

(b) the other person is under 13.

(2) A person guilty of an offence under this section is liable, on conviction on indictment, to imprisonment for life.

6 Assault of a child under 13 by penetration

(1) A person commits an offence if—

(a) he intentionally penetrates the vagina or anus of another person with a part of his body or anything else,

(b) the penetration is sexual, and

(c) the other person is under 13.

(2) A person guilty of an offence under this section is liable, on conviction on indictment, to imprisonment for life.

7 Sexual assault of a child under 13

(1) A person commits an offence if—

(a) he intentionally touches another person,

(b) the touching is sexual, and

(c) the other person is under 13.

(2) A person guilty of an offence under this section is liable—

(a) on summary conviction, to imprisonment for a term not exceeding 6 months or a fine not exceeding the statutory maximum or both;

(b) on conviction on indictment, to imprisonment for a term not exceeding 14 years.

8 Causing or inciting a child under 13 to engage in sexual activity

(1)   A person commits an offence if—

    (a)   he intentionally causes or incites another person (B) to engage in an activity,

    (b)   the activity is sexual, and

    (c)   B is under 13.

(2)   A person guilty of an offence under this section, if the activity caused or incited involved—

    (a)   penetration of B's anus or vagina,

    (b)   penetration of B's mouth with a person's penis,

    (c)   penetration of a person's anus or vagina with a part of B's body or by B with anything else, or

    (d)   penetration of a person's mouth with B's penis,

is liable, on conviction on indictment, to imprisonment for life.

(3)   Unless subsection (2) applies, a person guilty of an offence under this section is liable—

    (a)   on summary conviction, to imprisonment for a term not exceeding 6 months or to a fine not exceeding the statutory maximum or both;

    (b)   on conviction on indictment, to imprisonment for a term not exceeding 14 years.

CHILD SEX OFFENCES

9   **Sexual activity with a child**

(1)   A person aged 18 or over (A) commits an offence if—

    (a)   he intentionally touches another person (B),

    (b)   the touching is sexual, and

    (c)   either—

        (i)   B is under 16 and A does not reasonably believe that B is 16 or over, or

        (ii)   B is under 13.

(2)   A person guilty of an offence under this section, if the touching involved—

    (a)   penetration of B's anus or vagina with a part of A's body or anything else,

    (b)   penetration of B's mouth with A's penis,

    (c)   penetration of A's anus or vagina with a part of B's body, or

    (d)   penetration of A's mouth with B's penis,

is liable, on conviction on indictment, to imprisonment for a term not exceeding 14 years.

(3)   Unless subsection (2) applies, a person guilty of an offence under this section

is liable—

(a)   on summary conviction, to imprisonment for a term not exceeding 6 months or to a fine not exceeding the statutory maximum or both;

(b)   on conviction on indictment, to imprisonment for a term not exceeding 14 years.

10   Causing or inciting a child to engage in sexual activity

(1)   A person aged 18 or over (A) commits an offence if—

(a)   he intentionally causes or incites another person (B) to engage in an activity,

(b)   the activity is sexual, and

(c)   either—

(i)   B is under 16 and A does not reasonably believe that B is 16 or over, or

(ii)   B is under 13.

(2)   A person guilty of an offence under this section, if the activity caused or incited involved—

(a)   penetration of B's anus or vagina,

(b)   penetration of B's mouth with a person's penis,

(c)   penetration of a person's anus or vagina with a part of B's body or by B with anything else, or

(d)   penetration of a person's mouth with B's penis,

is liable, on conviction on indictment, to imprisonment for a term not exceeding 14 years.

(3)   Unless subsection (2) applies, a person guilty of an offence under this section is liable—

(a)   on summary conviction, to imprisonment for a term not exceeding 6 months or to a fine not exceeding the statutory maximum or both;

(b)   on conviction on indictment, to imprisonment for a term not exceeding 14 years.

11   Engaging in sexual activity in the presence of a child

(1)   A person aged 18 or over (A) commits an offence if—

(a)   he intentionally engages in an activity,

(b)   the activity is sexual,

(c)   for the purpose of obtaining sexual gratification, he engages in it—

(i)   when another person (B) is present or is in a place from which A can be observed, and

(ii)   knowing or believing that B is aware, or intending that B should be aware, that he is engaging in it, and

(d) either—

    (i) B is under 16 and A does not reasonably believe that B is 16 or over, or

    (ii) B is under 13.

(2) A person guilty of an offence under this section is liable—

(a) on summary conviction, to imprisonment for a term not exceeding 6 months or a fine not exceeding the statutory maximum or both;

(b) on conviction on indictment, to imprisonment for a term not exceeding 10 years.

12 Causing a child to watch a sexual act

(1) A person aged 18 or over (A) commits an offence if—

(a) for the purpose of obtaining sexual gratification, he intentionally causes another person (B) to watch a third person engaging in an activity, or to look at an image of any person engaging in an activity,

(b) the activity is sexual, and

(c) either—

    (i) B is under 16 and A does not reasonably believe that B is 16 or over, or

    (ii) B is under 13.

(2) A person guilty of an offence under this section is liable—

(a) on summary conviction, to imprisonment for a term not exceeding 6 months or a fine not exceeding the statutory maximum or both;

(b) on conviction on indictment, to imprisonment for a term not exceeding 10 years.

13 Child sex offences committed by children or young persons

(1) A person under 18 commits an offence if he does anything which would be an offence under any of sections 9 to 12 if he were aged 18.

(2) A person guilty of an offence under this section is liable—

(a) on summary conviction, to imprisonment for a term not exceeding 6 months or a fine not exceeding the statutory maximum or both;

(b) on conviction on indictment, to imprisonment for a term not exceeding 5 years.

14 Arranging or facilitating commission of a child sex offence

(1) A person commits an offence if—

(a) he intentionally arranges or facilitates something that he intends to do, intends another person to do, or believes that another person will do, in any part of the world, and

(b) doing it will involve the commission of an offence under any of sections 9 to 13.

(2)   A person does not commit an offence under this section if—

(a)   he arranges or facilitates something that he believes another person will do, but that he does not intend to do or intend another person to do, and

(b)   any offence within subsection (1)(b) would be an offence against a child for whose protection he acts.

(3)   For the purposes of subsection (2), a person acts for the protection of a child if he acts for the purpose of—

(a)   protecting the child from sexually transmitted infection,

(b)   protecting the physical safety of the child,

(c)   preventing the child from becoming pregnant, or

(d)   promoting the child's emotional well-being by the giving of advice,

and not for the purpose of obtaining sexual gratification or for the purpose of causing or encouraging the activity constituting the offence within subsection (1)(b) or the child's participation in it.

(4)   A person guilty of an offence under this section is liable—

(a)   on summary conviction, to imprisonment for a term not exceeding 6 months or a fine not exceeding the statutory maximum or both;

(b)   on conviction on indictment, to imprisonment for a term not exceeding 14 years.

15   **Meeting a child following sexual grooming etc.**

(1)   A person aged 18 or over (A) commits an offence if—

[(a)   A has met or communicated with another person (B) on at least two occasions and subsequently—

(i)   A intentionally meets B,

(ii)   A travels with the intention of meeting B in any part of the world or arranges to meet B in any part of the world, or

(iii)   B travels with the intention of meeting A in any part of the world,

(b)   A intends to do anything to or in respect of B, during or after the meeting mentioned in paragraph (a)(i) to (iii) and in any part of the world, which if done will involve the commission by A of a relevant offence,]

(c)   B is under 16, and

(d)   A does not reasonably believe that B is 16 or over.

(2)   In subsection (1)—

(a)   the reference to A having met or communicated with B is a reference to A having met B in any part of the world or having communicated with B by any means from, to or in any part of the world;

(b)   "relevant offence" means—

    (i)   an offence under this Part,

    (ii)   an offence within any of paragraphs 61 to 92 of Schedule 3, or

    (iii)   anything done outside England and Wales and Northern Ireland which is not an offence within sub-paragraph (i) or (ii) but would be an offence within sub-paragraph (i) if done in England and Wales.

(3)   In this section as it applies to Northern Ireland—

    (a)   subsection (1) has effect with the substitution of " 17" for "16" in both places;

    (b)   subsection (2)(b)(iii) has effect with the substitution of " sub-paragraph (ii) if done in Northern Ireland" for "sub-paragraph (i) if done in England and Wales".

(4)   A person guilty of an offence under this section is liable—

    (a)   on summary conviction, to imprisonment for a term not exceeding 6 months or a fine not exceeding the statutory maximum or both;

    (b)   on conviction on indictment, to imprisonment for a term not exceeding 10 years.

ABUSE OF POSITION OF TRUST

16   Abuse of position of trust: sexual activity with a child

(1)   A person aged 18 or over (A) commits an offence if—

    (a)   he intentionally touches another person (B),

    (b)   the touching is sexual,

    (c)   A is in a position of trust in relation to B,

    (d)   where subsection (2) applies, A knows or could reasonably be expected to know of the circumstances by virtue of which he is in a position of trust in relation to B, and

    (e)   either—

        (i)   B is under 18 and A does not reasonably believe that B is 18 or over, or

        (ii)   B is under 13.

(2)   This subsection applies where A—

    (a)   is in a position of trust in relation to B by virtue of circumstances within section 21(2), (3), (4) or (5), and

    (b)   is not in such a position of trust by virtue of other circumstances.

(3)   Where in proceedings for an offence under this section it is proved that the other person was under 18, the defendant is to be taken not to have

reasonably believed that that person was 18 or over unless sufficient evidence is adduced to raise an issue as to whether he reasonably believed it.

(4) Where in proceedings for an offence under this section—

    (a) it is proved that the defendant was in a position of trust in relation to the other person by virtue of circumstances within section 21(2), (3), (4) or (5), and

    (b) it is not proved that he was in such a position of trust by virtue of other circumstances,

it is to be taken that the defendant knew or could reasonably have been expected to know of the circumstances by virtue of which he was in such a position of trust unless sufficient evidence is adduced to raise an issue as to whether he knew or could reasonably have been expected to know of those circumstances.

(5) A person guilty of an offence under this section is liable—

    (a) on summary conviction, to imprisonment for a term not exceeding 6 months or a fine not exceeding the statutory maximum or both;

    (b) on conviction on indictment, to imprisonment for a term not exceeding 5 years.

17 Abuse of position of trust: causing or inciting a child to engage in sexual activity

(1) A person aged 18 or over (A) commits an offence if—

    (a) he intentionally causes or incites another person (B) to engage in an activity,

    (b) the activity is sexual,

    (c) A is in a position of trust in relation to B,

    (d) where subsection (2) applies, A knows or could reasonably be expected to know of the circumstances by virtue of which he is in a position of trust in relation to B, and

    (e) either—

        (i) B is under 18 and A does not reasonably believe that B is 18 or over, or

        (ii) B is under 13.

(2) This subsection applies where A—

    (a) is in a position of trust in relation to B by virtue of circumstances within section 21(2), (3), (4) or (5), and

    (b) is not in such a position of trust by virtue of other circumstances.

(3) Where in proceedings for an offence under this section it is proved that the other person was under 18, the defendant is to be taken not to have reasonably believed that that person was 18 or over unless sufficient evidence is adduced to raise an issue as to whether he reasonably believed it.

(4) Where in proceedings for an offence under this section—

(a)   it is proved that the defendant was in a position of trust in relation to the other person by virtue of circumstances within section 21(2), (3), (4) or (5), and

(b)   it is not proved that he was in such a position of trust by virtue of other circumstances,

it is to be taken that the defendant knew or could reasonably have been expected to know of the circumstances by virtue of which he was in such a position of trust unless sufficient evidence is adduced to raise an issue as to whether he knew or could reasonably have been expected to know of those circumstances.

(5)   A person guilty of an offence under this section is liable—

(a)   on summary conviction, to imprisonment for a term not exceeding 6 months or a fine not exceeding the statutory maximum or both;

(b)   on conviction on indictment, to imprisonment for a term not exceeding 5 years.

18   Abuse of position of trust: sexual activity in the presence of a child

(1)   A person aged 18 or over (A) commits an offence if—

(a)   he intentionally engages in an activity,

(b)   the activity is sexual,

(c)   for the purpose of obtaining sexual gratification, he engages in it—

(i)   when another person (B) is present or is in a place from which A can be observed, and

(ii)   knowing or believing that B is aware, or intending that B should be aware, that he is engaging in it,

(d)   A is in a position of trust in relation to B,

(e)   where subsection (2) applies, A knows or could reasonably be expected to know of the circumstances by virtue of which he is in a position of trust in relation to B, and

(f)   either—

(i)   B is under 18 and A does not reasonably believe that B is 18 or over, or

(ii)   B is under 13.

(2)   This subsection applies where A—

(a)   is in a position of trust in relation to B by virtue of circumstances within section 21(2), (3), (4) or (5), and

(b)   is not in such a position of trust by virtue of other circumstances.

(3)   Where in proceedings for an offence under this section it is proved that the other person was under 18, the defendant is to be taken not to have reasonably believed that that person was 18 or over unless sufficient evidence is adduced to raise an issue as to whether he reasonably believed it.

(4) Where in proceedings for an offence under this section—

    (a) it is proved that the defendant was in a position of trust in relation to the other person by virtue of circumstances within section 21(2), (3), (4) or (5), and

    (b) it is not proved that he was in such a position of trust by virtue of other circumstances,

it is to be taken that the defendant knew or could reasonably have been expected to know of the circumstances by virtue of which he was in such a position of trust unless sufficient evidence is adduced to raise an issue as to whether he knew or could reasonably have been expected to know of those circumstances.

(5) A person guilty of an offence under this section is liable—

    (a) on summary conviction, to imprisonment for a term not exceeding 6 months or a fine not exceeding the statutory maximum or both;

    (b) on conviction on indictment, to imprisonment for a term not exceeding 5 years.

19 Abuse of position of trust: causing a child to watch a sexual act

(1) A person aged 18 or over (A) commits an offence if—

    (a) for the purpose of obtaining sexual gratification, he intentionally causes another person (B) to watch a third person engaging in an activity, or to look at an image of any person engaging in an activity,

    (b) the activity is sexual,

    (c) A is in a position of trust in relation to B,

    (d) where subsection (2) applies, A knows or could reasonably be expected to know of the circumstances by virtue of which he is in a position of trust in relation to B, and

    (e) either—

        (i) B is under 18 and A does not reasonably believe that B is 18 or over, or

        (ii) B is under 13.

(2) This subsection applies where A—

    (a) is in a position of trust in relation to B by virtue of circumstances within section 21(2), (3), (4) or (5), and

    (b) is not in such a position of trust by virtue of other circumstances.

(3) Where in proceedings for an offence under this section it is proved that the other person was under 18, the defendant is to be taken not to have reasonably believed that that person was 18 or over unless sufficient evidence is adduced to raise an issue as to whether he reasonably believed it.

(4) Where in proceedings for an offence under this section—

    (a) it is proved that the defendant was in a position of trust in relation to the other person by virtue of circumstances within section 21(2), (3), (4) or (5), and

(b)　　　it is not proved that he was in such a position of trust by virtue of other circumstances,

it is to be taken that the defendant knew or could reasonably have been expected to know of the circumstances by virtue of which he was in such a position of trust unless sufficient evidence is adduced to raise an issue as to whether he knew or could reasonably have been expected to know of those circumstances.

(5)　　　A person guilty of an offence under this section is liable—

(a)　　　on summary conviction, to imprisonment for a term not exceeding 6 months or a fine not exceeding the statutory maximum or both;

(b)　　　on conviction on indictment, to imprisonment for a term not exceeding 5 years.

20　　Abuse of position of trust: acts done in Scotland

Anything which, if done in England and Wales or Northern Ireland, would constitute an offence under any of sections 16 to 19 also constitutes that offence if done in Scotland.

21　　Positions of trust

(1)　　　For the purposes of sections 16 to 19, a person (A) is in a position of trust in relation to another person (B) if—

(a)　　　any of the following subsections applies, or

(b)　　　any condition specified in an order made by the Secretary of State is met.

(2)　　　This subsection applies if A looks after persons under 18 who are detained in an institution by virtue of a court order or under an enactment, and B is so detained in that institution.

(3)　　　This subsection applies if A looks after persons under 18 who are resident in a home or other place in which—

(a)　　　accommodation and maintenance are provided by an authority [in accordance with section 22C(6)] of the Children Act 1989 (c. 41) or Article 27(2) of the Children (Northern Ireland) Order 1995 (S.I. 1995/755 (N.I. 2)), or

(b)　　　accommodation is provided by a voluntary organisation under section 59(1) of that Act or Article 75(1) of that Order,

and B is resident, and is so provided with accommodation and maintenance or accommodation, in that place.

(4)　　　This subsection applies if A looks after persons under 18 who are accommodated and cared for in one of the following institutions—

(a)　　　a hospital,

(b)   [in Wales,] an independent clinic,

(c)   a care home, residential care home or private hospital,

(d)   a community home, voluntary home or children's home,

(e)   a home provided under section 82(5) of the Children Act 1989, or

(f)   a residential family centre,

and B is accommodated and cared for in that institution.

(5)   This subsection applies if A looks after persons under 18 who are receiving education at an educational institution and B is receiving, and A is not receiving, education at that institution.

(6)   This subsection applies if A is appointed to be the guardian of B under Article 159 or 160 of the Children (Northern Ireland) Order 1995 (S.I. 1995/755 (N.I. 2)).

(7)   This subsection applies if A is engaged in the provision of services under, or pursuant to anything done under—

(a)   sections 8 to 10 of the Employment and Training Act 1973 (c. 50), or

[(b)   section 68, 70(1)(b) or 74 of the Education and Skills Act 2008,]

and, in that capacity, looks after B on an individual basis.

(8)   This subsection applies if A regularly has unsupervised contact with B (whether face to face or by any other means)—

(a)   in the exercise of functions of a local authority under section 20 or 21 of the Children Act 1989 (c. 41), or

(b)   in the exercise of functions of an authority under Article 21 or 23 of the Children (Northern Ireland) Order 1995.

(9)   This subsection applies if A, as a person who is to report to the court under section 7 of the Children Act 1989 or Article 4 of the Children (Northern Ireland) Order 1995 on matters relating to the welfare of B, regularly has unsupervised contact with B (whether face to face or by any other means).

(10)   This subsection applies if A is a personal adviser appointed for B under—

(a)   section 23B(2) of, or paragraph 19C of Schedule 2 to, the Children Act 1989, or

(b)   Article 34A(10) or 34C(2) of the Children (Northern Ireland) Order 1995,

and, in that capacity, looks after B on an individual basis.

(11)   This subsection applies if—

(a)   B is subject to a care order, a supervision order or an education supervision order, and

(b)   in the exercise of functions conferred by virtue of the order on an authorised person or the authority designated by the order, A looks after B on an individual basis.

(12)   This subsection applies if A—

    (a)   is an officer of the Service [or Welsh family proceedings officer (within the meaning given by section 35 of the Children Act 2004)] appointed for B under section 41(1) of the Children Act 1989,

    (b)   is appointed a children's guardian of B under rule 6 or rule 18 of the Adoption Rules 1984 (S.I. 1984/265), . . .

    (c)   is appointed to be the guardian ad litem of B under rule 9.5 of the Family Proceedings Rules 1991 (S. I. 1991/1247) or under Article 60(1) of the Children (Northern Ireland) Order 1995, [or

    (d)   is appointed to be the children's guardian of B under rule 59 of the Family Procedure (Adoption) Rules 2005 (S.I. 2005/2795) or rule 16.3(1)(ii) or rule 16.4 of the Family Procedure Rules 2010 (S.I. 2010/2955),]

and, in that capacity, regularly has unsupervised contact with B (whether face to face or by any other means).

(13)   This subsection applies if—

    (a)   B is subject to requirements imposed by or under an enactment on his release from detention for a criminal offence, or is subject to requirements imposed by a court order made in criminal proceedings, and

    (b)   A looks after B on an individual basis in pursuance of the requirements.

22   Positions of trust: interpretation

(1)   The following provisions apply for the purposes of section 21.

(2)   Subject to subsection (3), a person looks after persons under 18 if he is regularly involved in caring for, training, supervising or being in sole charge of such persons.

(3)   A person (A) looks after another person (B) on an individual basis if—

    (a)   A is regularly involved in caring for, training or supervising B, and

    (b)   in the course of his involvement, A regularly has unsupervised contact with B (whether face to face or by any other means).

(4)   A person receives education at an educational institution if—

    (a)   he is registered or otherwise enrolled as a pupil or student at the institution, or

    (b)   he receives education at the institution under arrangements with another educational institution at which he is so registered or otherwise enrolled.

(5)   In section 21—

"authority"—

    (a)   in relation to England and Wales, means a local authority;

    (b)   in relation to Northern Ireland, has the meaning given by Article 2(2) of the Children (Northern Ireland) Order 1995 (S.I. 1995/755 (N.I. 2));

"care home" means an establishment which is a care home for the purposes of the Care Standards Act 2000 (c. 14);

"care order" has—

    (a)   in relation to England and Wales, the same meaning as in the Children Act 1989 (c. 41), and

    (b)   in relation to Northern Ireland, the same meaning as in the Children (Northern Ireland) Order 1995;

"children's home" has—

    (a)   in relation to England and Wales, the meaning given by section 1 of the Care Standards Act 2000, and

    (b)   in relation to Northern Ireland, the meaning that would be given by Article 9 of the Health and Personal Social Services (Quality, Improvement and Regulation) (Northern Ireland) Order 2003 (S.I. 2003/431 (N.I. 9)) ("the 2003 Order") if in paragraph (4) of that Article sub-paragraphs (d), (f) and (g) were omitted;

"community home" has the meaning given by section 53 of the Children Act 1989;

"education supervision order" has—

    (a)   in relation to England and Wales, the meaning given by section 36 of the Children Act 1989, and

    (b)   in relation to Northern Ireland, the meaning given by Article 49(1) of the Children (Northern Ireland) Order 1995;

["hospital" means—

    (a)   a hospital as defined by section 275 of the National Health Service Act 2006, or section 206 of the National Health Service (Wales) Act 2006; or

    (b)   any other establishment—

        (i)   in England, in which any of the services listed in subsection (6) are provided; and

        (ii)   in Wales, which is a hospital within the meaning given by section 2(3) of the Care Standards Act 2000;]

"independent clinic" has—

    (a)   . . . the meaning given by section 2 of the Care Standards Act 2000;

    (b)   in relation to Northern Ireland, the meaning given by Article 2(2) of the 2003 Order;

"private hospital" has the meaning given by Article 90(2) of the Mental Health (Northern Ireland) Order 1986 (S.I. 1986/595 (N.I. 4));

"residential care home" means an establishment which is a residential care home for the purposes of the 2003 Order;

"residential family centre" has the meaning given by section 22 of the Health and Personal Social Services Act (Northern Ireland) 2001 (c. 3);

"supervision order" has—

(a) in relation to England and Wales, the meaning given by section 31(11) of the Children Act 1989 (c. 41), and

(b) in relation to Northern Ireland, the meaning given by Article 49(1) of the Children (Northern Ireland) Order 1995 (S.I. 1995/ 755 (N.I. 2));

"voluntary home" has—

(a) in relation to England and Wales, the meaning given by section 60(3) of the Children Act 1989, and

(b) in relation to Northern Ireland, the meaning given by Article 74(1) of the Children (Northern Ireland) Order 1995.

[(6)   In subsection (5), in the definition of "independent medical agency", "undertaking" includes any business or profession and—

(a) in relation to a public or local authority, includes the exercise of any functions of that authority; and

(b) in relation to any other body of persons, whether corporate or unincorporate, includes any of the activities of that body.]

23 Sections 16 to 19: [exception for spouses and civil partners]

(1) Conduct by a person (A) which would otherwise be an offence under any of sections 16 to 19 against another person (B) is not an offence under that section if at the time —

(a) B is 16 or over, and

(b) A and B are lawfully married [or civil partners of each other].

(2) In proceedings for such an offence it is for the defendant to prove that A and B [were at the time lawfully married or civil partners of each other].

24 Sections 16 to 19: sexual relationships which pre-date position of trust

(1) Conduct by a person (A) which would otherwise be an offence under any of sections 16 to 19 against another person (B) is not an offence under that section if, immediately before the position of trust arose, a sexual relationship existed between A and B.

(2) Subsection (1) does not apply if at that time sexual intercourse between A and B would have been unlawful.

(3) In proceedings for an offence under any of sections 16 to 19 it is for the defendant to prove that such a relationship existed at that time.

FAMILIAL CHILD SEX OFFENCES

25 Sexual activity with a child family member

(1) A person (A) commits an offence if—

(a)　　he intentionally touches another person (B),

(b)　　the touching is sexual,

(c)　　the relation of A to B is within section 27,

(d)　　A knows or could reasonably be expected to know that his relation to B is of a description falling within that section, and

(e)　　either—

　　　　(i)　　B is under 18 and A does not reasonably believe that B is 18 or over, or

　　　　(ii)　　B is under 13.

(2)　　Where in proceedings for an offence under this section it is proved that the other person was under 18, the defendant is to be taken not to have reasonably believed that that person was 18 or over unless sufficient evidence is adduced to raise an issue as to whether he reasonably believed it.

(3)　　Where in proceedings for an offence under this section it is proved that the relation of the defendant to the other person was of a description falling within section 27, it is to be taken that the defendant knew or could reasonably have been expected to know that his relation to the other person was of that description unless sufficient evidence is adduced to raise an issue as to whether he knew or could reasonably have been expected to know that it was.

(4)　　A person guilty of an offence under this section, if aged 18 or over at the time of the offence, is liable—

(a)　　where subsection (6) applies, on conviction on indictment to imprisonment for a term not exceeding 14 years;

(b)　　in any other case—

　　　　(i)　　on summary conviction, to imprisonment for a term not exceeding 6 months or a fine not exceeding the statutory maximum or both;

　　　　(ii)　　on conviction on indictment, to imprisonment for a term not exceeding 14 years.

(5)　　Unless subsection (4) applies, a person guilty of an offence under this section is liable—

(a)　　on summary conviction, to imprisonment for a term not exceeding 6 months or a fine not exceeding the statutory maximum or both;

(b)　　on conviction on indictment, to imprisonment for a term not exceeding 5 years.

(6)　　This subsection applies where the touching involved—

(a)　　penetration of B's anus or vagina with a part of A's body or anything else,

(b)　　penetration of B's mouth with A's penis,

(c)　　penetration of A's anus or vagina with a part of B's body, or

(d)   penetration of A's mouth with B's penis.

26   **Inciting a child family member to engage in sexual activity**

(1)   A person (A) commits an offence if—

(a)   he intentionally incites another person (B) to touch, or allow himself to be touched by, A,

(b)   the touching is sexual,

(c)   the relation of A to B is within section 27,

(d)   A knows or could reasonably be expected to know that his relation to B is of a description falling within that section, and

(e)   either—

(i)   B is under 18 and A does not reasonably believe that B is 18 or over, or

(ii)   B is under 13.

(2)   Where in proceedings for an offence under this section it is proved that the other person was under 18, the defendant is to be taken not to have reasonably believed that that person was 18 or over unless sufficient evidence is adduced to raise an issue as to whether he reasonably believed it.

(3)   Where in proceedings for an offence under this section it is proved that the relation of the defendant to the other person was of a description falling within section 27, it is to be taken that the defendant knew or could reasonably have been expected to know that his relation to the other person was of that description unless sufficient evidence is adduced to raise an issue as to whether he knew or could reasonably have been expected to know that it was.

(4)   A person guilty of an offence under this section, if he was aged 18 or over at the time of the offence, is liable—

(a)   where subsection (6) applies, on conviction on indictment to imprisonment for a term not exceeding 14 years;

(b)   in any other case—

(i)   on summary conviction, to imprisonment for a term not exceeding 6 months or a fine not exceeding the statutory maximum or both;

(ii)   on conviction on indictment, to imprisonment for a term not exceeding 14 years.

(5)   Unless subsection (4) applies, a person guilty of an offence under this section is liable—

(a)   on summary conviction, to imprisonment for a term not exceeding 6 months or a fine not exceeding the statutory maximum or both;

(b)   on conviction on indictment, to imprisonment for a term not exceeding 5 years.

(6)   This subsection applies where the touching to which the incitement related involved—

    (a)   penetration of B's anus or vagina with a part of A's body or anything else,

    (b)   penetration of B's mouth with A's penis,

    (c)   penetration of A's anus or vagina with a part of B's body, or

    (d)   penetration of A's mouth with B's penis.

27 Family relationships

(1)   The relation of one person (A) to another (B) is within this section if—

    (a)   it is within any of subsections (2) to (4), or

    (b)   it would be within one of those subsections but for [section 39 of the Adoption Act 1976 or] section 67 of the Adoption and Children Act 2002 (c. 38) (status conferred by adoption).

(2)   The relation of A to B is within this subsection if—

    (a)   one of them is the other's parent, grandparent, brother, sister, half-brother, half-sister, aunt or uncle, or

    (b)   A is or has been B's foster parent.

(3)   The relation of A to B is within this subsection if A and B live or have lived in the same household, or A is or has been regularly involved in caring for, training, supervising or being in sole charge of B, and—

    (a)   one of them is or has been the other's step-parent,

    (b)   A and B are cousins,

    (c)   one of them is or has been the other's stepbrother or stepsister, or

    (d)   the parent or present or former foster parent of one of them is or has been the other's foster parent.

(4)   The relation of A to B is within this subsection if—

    (a)   A and B live in the same household, and

    (b)   A is regularly involved in caring for, training, supervising or being in sole charge of B.

(5)   For the purposes of this section—

    (a)   "aunt" means the sister or half-sister of a person's parent, and "uncle" has a corresponding meaning;

    (b)   "cousin" means the child of an aunt or uncle;

    (c)   a person is a child's foster parent if—

        [(i)   he is a person with whom the child has been placed under section 22C of the Children Act 1989 in a placement falling within subsection (6)(a) or (b) of that section (placement with local authority foster parent),

        (ia)   he is a person with whom the child has been placed under section 59(1)(a) of that Act (placement by voluntary organisation),]

  (ii) he fosters the child privately, within the meaning given by section 66(1)(b) of that Act;

 (d) a person is another's partner (whether they are of different sexes or the same sex) if they live together as partners in an enduring family relationship;

 (e) "step-parent" includes a parent's partner and "stepbrother" and "stepsister" include the child of a parent's partner.

28 Sections 25 and 26: [exception for spouses and civil partners]

 (1) Conduct by a person (A) which would otherwise be an offence under section 25 or 26 against another person (B) is not an offence under that section if at the time—

  (a) B is 16 or over, and

  (b) A and B are lawfully married [or civil partners of each other].

 (2) In proceedings for such an offence it is for the defendant to prove that A and B [were at the time lawfully married or civil partners of each other].

29 Sections 25 and 26: sexual relationships which pre-date family relationships

 (1) Conduct by a person (A) which would otherwise be an offence under section 25 or 26 against another person (B) is not an offence under that section if—

  (a) the relation of A to B is not within subsection (2) of section 27,

  (b) it would not be within that subsection if [section 39 of the Adoption Act 1976 or] section 67 of the Adoption and Children Act 2002 (c. 38) did not apply, and

  (c) immediately before the relation of A to B first became such as to fall within section 27, a sexual relationship existed between A and B.

 (2) Subsection (1) does not apply if at the time referred to in subsection (1)(c) sexual intercourse between A and B would have been unlawful.

 (3) In proceedings for an offence under section 25 or 26 it is for the defendant to prove the matters mentioned in subsection (1)(a) to (c).

OFFENCES AGAINST PERSONS WITH A MENTAL DISORDER IMPEDING CHOICE

30 Sexual activity with a person with a mental disorder impeding choice

 (1) A person (A) commits an offence if—

  (a) he intentionally touches another person (B),

  (b) the touching is sexual,

  (c) B is unable to refuse because of or for a reason related to a mental disorder, and

(d)   A knows or could reasonably be expected to know that B has a mental disorder and that because of it or for a reason related to it B is likely to be unable to refuse.

(2)   B is unable to refuse if—

    (a)   he lacks the capacity to choose whether to agree to the touching (whether because he lacks sufficient understanding of the nature or reasonably foreseeable consequences of what is being done, or for any other reason), or

    (b)   he is unable to communicate such a choice to A.

(3)   A person guilty of an offence under this section, if the touching involved—

    (a)   penetration of B's anus or vagina with a part of A's body or anything else,

    (b)   penetration of B's mouth with A's penis,

    (c)   penetration of A's anus or vagina with a part of B's body, or

    (d)   penetration of A's mouth with B's penis,

is liable, on conviction on indictment, to imprisonment for life.

(4)   Unless subsection (3) applies, a person guilty of an offence under this section is liable—

    (a)   on summary conviction, to imprisonment for a term not exceeding 6 months or to a fine not exceeding the statutory maximum or both;

    (b)   on conviction on indictment, to imprisonment for a term not exceeding 14 years.

31   Causing or inciting a person, with a mental disorder impeding choice, to engage in sexual activity

(1)   A person (A) commits an offence if—

    (a)   he intentionally causes or incites another person (B) to engage in an activity,

    (b)   the activity is sexual,

    (c)   B is unable to refuse because of or for a reason related to a mental disorder, and

    (d)   A knows or could reasonably be expected to know that B has a mental disorder and that because of it or for a reason related to it B is likely to be unable to refuse.

(2)   B is unable to refuse if—

    (a)   he lacks the capacity to choose whether to agree to engaging in the activity caused or incited (whether because he lacks sufficient understanding of the nature or reasonably foreseeable consequences of the activity, or for any other reason), or

    (b)   he is unable to communicate such a choice to A.

(3)   A person guilty of an offence under this section, if the activity caused or

incited involved—

(a)   penetration of B's anus or vagina,

(b)   penetration of B's mouth with a person's penis,

(c)   penetration of a person's anus or vagina with a part of B's body or by B with anything else, or

(d)   penetration of a person's mouth with B's penis,

is liable, on conviction on indictment, to imprisonment for life.

(4)   Unless subsection (3) applies, a person guilty of an offence under this section is liable—

(a)   on summary conviction, to imprisonment for a term not exceeding 6 months or to a fine not exceeding the statutory maximum or both;

(b)   on conviction on indictment, to imprisonment for a term not exceeding 14 years.

32 Engaging in sexual activity in the presence of a person with a mental disorder impeding choice

(1)   A person (A) commits an offence if—

(a)   he intentionally engages in an activity,

(b)   the activity is sexual,

(c)   for the purpose of obtaining sexual gratification, he engages in it—

(i)   when another person (B) is present or is in a place from which A can be observed, and

(ii)   knowing or believing that B is aware, or intending that B should be aware, that he is engaging in it,

(d)   B is unable to refuse because of or for a reason related to a mental disorder, and

(e)   A knows or could reasonably be expected to know that B has a mental disorder and that because of it or for a reason related to it B is likely to be unable to refuse.

(2)   B is unable to refuse if—

(a)   he lacks the capacity to choose whether to agree to being present (whether because he lacks sufficient understanding of the nature of the activity, or for any other reason), or

(b)   he is unable to communicate such a choice to A.

(3)   A person guilty of an offence under this section is liable—

(a)   on summary conviction, to imprisonment for a term not exceeding 6 months or a fine not exceeding the statutory maximum or both;

(b)   on conviction on indictment, to imprisonment for a term not exceeding 10 years.

33 Causing a person, with a mental disorder impeding choice, to watch a sexual act

(1) A person (A) commits an offence if—

    (a) for the purpose of obtaining sexual gratification, he intentionally causes another person (B) to watch a third person engaging in an activity, or to look at an image of any person engaging in an activity,

    (b) the activity is sexual,

    (c) B is unable to refuse because of or for a reason related to a mental disorder, and

    (d) A knows or could reasonably be expected to know that B has a mental disorder and that because of it or for a reason related to it B is likely to be unable to refuse.

(2) B is unable to refuse if—

    (a) he lacks the capacity to choose whether to agree to watching or looking (whether because he lacks sufficient understanding of the nature of the activity, or for any other reason), or

    (b) he is unable to communicate such a choice to A.

(3) A person guilty of an offence under this section is liable—

    (a) on summary conviction, to imprisonment for a term not exceeding 6 months or a fine not exceeding the statutory maximum or both;

    (b) on conviction on indictment, to imprisonment for a term not exceeding 10 years.

INDUCEMENTS ETC. TO PERSONS WITH A MENTAL DISORDER

34 Inducement, threat or deception to procure sexual activity with a person with a mental disorder

(1) A person (A) commits an offence if—

    (a) with the agreement of another person (B) he intentionally touches that person,

    (b) the touching is sexual,

    (c) A obtains B's agreement by means of an inducement offered or given, a threat made or a deception practised by A for that purpose,

    (d) B has a mental disorder, and

    (e) A knows or could reasonably be expected to know that B has a mental disorder.

(2) A person guilty of an offence under this section, if the touching involved—

    (a) penetration of B's anus or vagina with a part of A's body or anything else,

    (b) penetration of B's mouth with A's penis,

    (c) penetration of A's anus or vagina with a part of B's body, or

    (d) penetration of A's mouth with B's penis,

is liable, on conviction on indictment, to imprisonment for life.

(3)　Unless subsection (2) applies, a person guilty of an offence under this section is liable—

(a)　on summary conviction, to imprisonment for a term not exceeding 6 months or a fine not exceeding the statutory maximum or both;

(b)　on conviction on indictment, to imprisonment for a term not exceeding 14 years.

35 Causing a person with a mental disorder to engage in or agree to engage in sexual activity by inducement, threat or deception

(1)　A person (A) commits an offence if—

(a)　by means of an inducement offered or given, a threat made or a deception practised by him for this purpose, he intentionally causes another person (B) to engage in, or to agree to engage in, an activity,

(b)　the activity is sexual,

(c)　B has a mental disorder, and

(d)　A knows or could reasonably be expected to know that B has a mental disorder.

(2)　A person guilty of an offence under this section, if the activity caused or agreed to involved—

(a)　penetration of B's anus or vagina,

(b)　penetration of B's mouth with a person's penis,

(c)　penetration of a person's anus or vagina with a part of B's body or by B with anything else, or

(d)　penetration of a person's mouth with B's penis,

is liable, on conviction on indictment, to imprisonment for life.

(3)　Unless subsection (2) applies, a person guilty of an offence under this section is liable—

(a)　on summary conviction, to imprisonment for a term not exceeding 6 months or a fine not exceeding the statutory maximum or both;

(b)　on conviction on indictment, to imprisonment for a term not exceeding 14 years.

36 Engaging in sexual activity in the presence, procured by inducement, threat or deception, of a person with a mental disorder

(1)　A person (A) commits an offence if—

(a)　he intentionally engages in an activity,

(b)　the activity is sexual,

(c)　for the purpose of obtaining sexual gratification, he engages in it—

(i)　when another person (B) is present or is in a place from which A can be observed, and

        (ii)   knowing or believing that B is aware, or intending that B should be aware, that he is engaging in it,

    (d)   B agrees to be present or in the place referred to in paragraph (c)(i) because of an inducement offered or given, a threat made or a deception practised by A for the purpose of obtaining that agreement,

    (e)   B has a mental disorder, and

    (f)   A knows or could reasonably be expected to know that B has a mental disorder.

(2)   A person guilty of an offence under this section is liable—

    (a)   on summary conviction, to imprisonment for a term not exceeding 6 months or a fine not exceeding the statutory maximum or both;

    (b)   on conviction on indictment, to imprisonment for a term not exceeding 10 years.

37   Causing a person with a mental disorder to watch a sexual act by inducement, threat or deception

(1)   A person (A) commits an offence if—

    (a)   for the purpose of obtaining sexual gratification, he intentionally causes another person (B) to watch a third person engaging in an activity, or to look at an image of any person engaging in an activity,

    (b)   the activity is sexual,

    (c)   B agrees to watch or look because of an inducement offered or given, a threat made or a deception practised by A for the purpose of obtaining that agreement,

    (d)   B has a mental disorder, and

    (e)   A knows or could reasonably be expected to know that B has a mental disorder.

(2)   A person guilty of an offence under this section is liable—

    (a)   on summary conviction, to imprisonment for a term not exceeding 6 months or a fine not exceeding the statutory maximum or both;

    (b)   on conviction on indictment, to imprisonment for a term not exceeding 10 years.

CARE WORKERS FOR PERSONS WITH A MENTAL DISORDER

38   Care workers: sexual activity with a person with a mental disorder

(1)   A person (A) commits an offence if—

    (a)   he intentionally touches another person (B),

    (b)   the touching is sexual,

    (c)   B has a mental disorder,

(d)   A knows or could reasonably be expected to know that B has a mental disorder, and

(e)   A is involved in B's care in a way that falls within section 42.

(2)   Where in proceedings for an offence under this section it is proved that the other person had a mental disorder, it is to be taken that the defendant knew or could reasonably have been expected to know that that person had a mental disorder unless sufficient evidence is adduced to raise an issue as to whether he knew or could reasonably have been expected to know it.

(3)   A person guilty of an offence under this section, if the touching involved—

(a)   penetration of B's anus or vagina with a part of A's body or anything else,

(b)   penetration of B's mouth with A's penis,

(c)   penetration of A's anus or vagina with a part of B's body, or

(d)   penetration of A's mouth with B's penis,

is liable, on conviction on indictment, to imprisonment for a term not exceeding 14 years.

(4)   Unless subsection (3) applies, a person guilty of an offence under this section is liable—

(a)   on summary conviction, to imprisonment for a term not exceeding 6 months or a fine not exceeding the statutory maximum or both;

(b)   on conviction on indictment, to imprisonment for a term not exceeding 10 years.

39   Care workers: causing or inciting sexual activity

(1)   A person (A) commits an offence if—

(a)   he intentionally causes or incites another person (B) to engage in an activity,

(b)   the activity is sexual,

(c)   B has a mental disorder,

(d)   A knows or could reasonably be expected to know that B has a mental disorder, and

(e)   A is involved in B's care in a way that falls within section 42.

(2)   Where in proceedings for an offence under this section it is proved that the other person had a mental disorder, it is to be taken that the defendant knew or could reasonably have been expected to know that that person had a mental disorder unless sufficient evidence is adduced to raise an issue as to whether he knew or could reasonably have been expected to know it.

(3)   A person guilty of an offence under this section, if the activity caused or incited involved—

(a)   penetration of B's anus or vagina,

(b) penetration of B's mouth with a person's penis,

(c) penetration of a person's anus or vagina with a part of B's body or by B with anything else, or

(d) penetration of a person's mouth with B's penis,

is liable, on conviction on indictment, to imprisonment for a term not exceeding 14 years.

(4) Unless subsection (3) applies, a person guilty of an offence under this section is liable—

(a) on summary conviction, to imprisonment for a term not exceeding 6 months or a fine not exceeding the statutory maximum or both;

(b) on conviction on indictment, to imprisonment for a term not exceeding 10 years.

40 Care workers: sexual activity in the presence of a person with a mental disorder

(1) A person (A) commits an offence if—

(a) he intentionally engages in an activity,

(b) the activity is sexual,

(c) for the purpose of obtaining sexual gratification, he engages in it—

(i) when another person (B) is present or is in a place from which A can be observed, and

(ii) knowing or believing that B is aware, or intending that B should be aware, that he is engaging in it,

(d) B has a mental disorder,

(e) A knows or could reasonably be expected to know that B has a mental disorder, and

(f) A is involved in B's care in a way that falls within section 42.

(2) Where in proceedings for an offence under this section it is proved that the other person had a mental disorder, it is to be taken that the defendant knew or could reasonably have been expected to know that that person had a mental disorder unless sufficient evidence is adduced to raise an issue as to whether he knew or could reasonably have been expected to know it.

(3) A person guilty of an offence under this section is liable—

(a) on summary conviction, to imprisonment for a term not exceeding 6 months or a fine not exceeding the statutory maximum or both;

(b) on conviction on indictment, to imprisonment for a term not exceeding 7 years.

41 Care workers: causing a person with a mental disorder to watch a sexual act

(1) A person (A) commits an offence if—

(a) for the purpose of obtaining sexual gratification, he intentionally causes another person (B) to watch a third person engaging in an activity, or to look at an image of any person engaging in an activity,

(b)   the activity is sexual,

(c)   B has a mental disorder,

(d)   A knows or could reasonably be expected to know that B has a mental disorder, and

(e)   A is involved in B's care in a way that falls within section 42.

(2)   Where in proceedings for an offence under this section it is proved that the other person had a mental disorder, it is to be taken that the defendant knew or could reasonably have been expected to know that that person had a mental disorder unless sufficient evidence is adduced to raise an issue as to whether he knew or could reasonably have been expected to know it.

(3)   A person guilty of an offence under this section is liable—

(a)   on summary conviction, to imprisonment for a term not exceeding 6 months or a fine not exceeding the statutory maximum or both;

(b)   on conviction on indictment, to imprisonment for a term not exceeding 7 years.

42   Care workers: interpretation

(1)   For the purposes of sections 38 to 41, a person (A) is involved in the care of another person (B) in a way that falls within this section if any of subsections (2) to (4) applies.

(2)   This subsection applies if—

(a)   B is accommodated and cared for in a care home, community home, voluntary home or children's home, and

(b)   A has functions to perform in the home in the course of employment which have brought him or are likely to bring him into regular face to face contact with B.

[(3)   This subsection applies if B is a patient for whom services are provided—

(a)   by a National Health Service body or an independent medical agency;

(b)   in an independent hospital; or

(c)   in Wales, in an independent clinic,

and A has functions to perform for the body or agency or in the hospital or clinic in the course of employment which have brought A or are likely to bring A into regular face to face contact with B.]

(4)   This subsection applies if A—

(a)   is, whether or not in the course of employment, a provider of care, assistance or services to B in connection with B's mental disorder, and

(b)   as such, has had or is likely to have regular face to face contact with B.

(5)   In this section—

"care home" means an establishment which is a care home for the purposes of the Care Standards Act 2000 (c. 14);

"children's home" has the meaning given by section 1 of that Act;

"community home" has the meaning given by section 53 of the Children Act 1989 (c. 41);

"employment" means any employment, whether paid or unpaid and whether under a contract of service or apprenticeship, under a contract for services, or otherwise than under a contract;

["independent clinic" has the meaning given by section 2 of the Care Standards Act 2000;

"independent hospital"

    (a) in England, means—

        (i) a hospital as defined by section 275 of the National Health Service Act 2006 that is not a health service hospital as defined by that section; or

        (ii) any other establishment in which any of the services listed in section 22(6) are provided and which is not a health service hospital as so defined; and

    (b) in Wales, has the meaning given by section 2 of the Care Standards Act 2000;

"independent medical agency"means an undertaking (not being an independent hospital, or in Wales an independent clinic) which consists of or includes the provision of services by medical practitioners;]

"National Health Service body" means—

    (a) a [Local Health Board] ,

    (b) a National Health Service trust,

    (ba) [the Secretary of State in relation to the exercise of functions under section 2A or 2B of, or paragraph 7C, 8 or 12 of Schedule 1 to, the National Health Service Act 2006,

    (bb) a local authority in relation to the exercise of functions under section 2B or 111 of, or any of paragraphs 1 to 7B, or 13 of Schedule 1 to, the National Health Service Act 2006,]

    (c) . . . .

    (d) a Special Health Authority;

"voluntary home" has the meaning given by section 60(3) of the Children Act 1989.

[(6)   In subsection (5), in the definition of "independent medical agency", "undertaking" includes any business or profession and—

(a)   in relation to a public or local authority, includes the exercise of any functions of that authority; and

(b)   in relation to any other body of persons, whether corporate or unincorporate, includes any of the activities of that body.]

43   Sections 38 to 41: [exception for spouses and civil partners]

(1)   Conduct by a person (A) which would otherwise be an offence under any of sections 38 to 41 against another person (B) is not an offence under that section if at the time—

(a)   B is 16 or over, and

(b)   A and B are lawfully married [or civil partners of each other].

(2)   In proceedings for such an offence it is for the defendant to prove that A and B [were at the time lawfully married or civil partners of each other].

PART 1
SEXUAL OFFENCES

ABUSE OF CHILDREN THROUGH PROSTITUTION AND PORNOGRAPHY

47   Paying for sexual services of a child

(1)   A person (A) commits an offence if—

(a)   he intentionally obtains for himself the sexual services of another person (B),

(b)   before obtaining those services, he has made or promised payment for those services to B or a third person, or knows that another person has made or promised such a payment, and

(c)   either—

(i)   B is under 18, and A does not reasonably believe that B is 18 or over, or

(ii)   B is under 13.

(2)   In this section, "payment" means any financial advantage, including the discharge of an obligation to pay or the provision of goods or services (including sexual services) gratuitously or at a discount.

(3)   A person guilty of an offence under this section against a person under 13, where subsection (6) applies, is liable on conviction on indictment to imprisonment for life.

(4)   Unless subsection (3) applies, a person guilty of an offence under this section against a person under 16 is liable—

(a)   where subsection (6) applies, on conviction on indictment, to imprisonment for a term not exceeding 14 years;

(b)   in any other case—

    (i)   on summary conviction, to imprisonment for a term not exceeding 6 months or a fine not exceeding the statutory maximum or both;

    (ii)   on conviction on indictment, to imprisonment for a term not exceeding 14 years.

(5)   Unless subsection (3) or (4) applies, a person guilty of an offence under this section is liable—

(a)   on summary conviction, to imprisonment for a term not exceeding 6 months or a fine not exceeding the statutory maximum or both;

(b)   on conviction on indictment, to imprisonment for a term not exceeding 7 years.

(6)   This subsection applies where the offence involved—

(a)   penetration of B's anus or vagina with a part of A's body or anything else,

(b)   penetration of B's mouth with A's penis,

(c)   penetration of A's anus or vagina with a part of B's body or by B with anything else, or

(d)   penetration of A's mouth with B's penis.

(7)   In the application of this section to Northern Ireland, subsection (4) has effect with the substitution of " 17" for "16".

48   Causing or inciting child prostitution or pornography

(1)   A person (A) commits an offence if—

(a)   he intentionally causes or incites another person (B) to become a prostitute, or to be involved in pornography, in any part of the world, and

(b)   either—

    (i)   B is under 18, and A does not reasonably believe that B is 18 or over, or

    (ii)   B is under 13.

(2)   A person guilty of an offence under this section is liable—

(a)   on summary conviction, to imprisonment for a term not exceeding 6 months or a fine not exceeding the statutory maximum or both;

(b)   on conviction on indictment, to imprisonment for a term not exceeding 14 years.

49   Controlling a child prostitute or a child involved in pornography

(1)   A person (A) commits an offence if—

(a)   he intentionally controls any of the activities of another person (B) relating to B's prostitution or involvement in pornography in any part of the world, and

(b)   either—

(i)   B is under 18, and A does not reasonably believe that B is 18 or over, or

(ii)   B is under 13.

(2)   A person guilty of an offence under this section is liable—

(a)   on summary conviction, to imprisonment for a term not exceeding 6 months or a fine not exceeding the statutory maximum or both;

(b)   on conviction on indictment, to imprisonment for a term not exceeding 14 years.

50   Arranging or facilitating child prostitution or pornography

(1)   A person (A) commits an offence if—

(a)   he intentionally arranges or facilitates the prostitution or involvement in pornography in any part of the world of another person (B), and

(b)   either—

(i)   B is under 18, and A does not reasonably believe that B is 18 or over, or

(ii)   B is under 13.

(2)   A person guilty of an offence under this section is liable—

(a)   on summary conviction, to imprisonment for a term not exceeding 6 months or a fine not exceeding the statutory maximum or both;

(b)   on conviction on indictment, to imprisonment for a term not exceeding 14 years.

51   Sections 48 to 50: interpretation

(1)   For the purposes of sections 48 to 50, a person is involved in pornography if an indecent image of that person is recorded; and similar expressions, and "pornography", are to be interpreted accordingly.

(2)   In those sections "prostitute" means a person (A) who, on at least one occasion and whether or not compelled to do so, offers or provides sexual services to another person in return for payment or a promise of payment to A or a third person; and "prostitution" is to be interpreted accordingly.

(3)   In subsection (2), "payment" means any financial advantage, including the discharge of an obligation to pay or the provision of goods or services (including sexual services) gratuitously or at a discount.

[51A   Soliciting

(1)   It is an offence for a person in a street or public place to solicit another (B) for the purpose of obtaining B's sexual services as a prostitute.

(2)   The reference to a person in a street or public place includes a person in a

vehicle in a street or public place.

(3)   A person guilty of an offence under this section is liable on summary conviction to a fine not exceeding level 3 on the standard scale.

(4)   In this section "street" has the meaning given by section 1(4) of the Street Offences Act 1959.]

EXPLOITATION OF PROSTITUTION

52   Causing or inciting prostitution for gain

(1)   A person commits an offence if—

    (a)   he intentionally causes or incites another person to become a prostitute in any part of the world, and

    (b)   he does so for or in the expectation of gain for himself or a third person.

(2)   A person guilty of an offence under this section is liable—

    (a)   on summary conviction, to imprisonment for a term not exceeding 6 months or a fine not exceeding the statutory maximum or both;

    (b)   on conviction on indictment, to imprisonment for a term not exceeding 7 years.

53   Controlling prostitution for gain

(1)   A person commits an offence if—

    (a)   he intentionally controls any of the activities of another person relating to that person's prostitution in any part of the world, and

    (b)   he does so for or in the expectation of gain for himself or a third person.

(2)   A person guilty of an offence under this section is liable—

    (a)   on summary conviction, to imprisonment for a term not exceeding 6 months or a fine not exceeding the statutory maximum or both;

    (b)   on conviction on indictment, to imprisonment for a term not exceeding 7 years.

[53A   Paying for sexual services of a prostitute subjected to force etc.

(1)   A person (A) commits an offence if—

    (a)   A makes or promises payment for the sexual services of a prostitute (B),

    (b)   a third person (C) has engaged in exploitative conduct of a kind likely to induce or encourage B to provide the sexual services for which A has made or promised payment, and

    (c)   C engaged in that conduct for or in the expectation of gain for C or another person (apart from A or B).

(2)   The following are irrelevant—

(a)   where in the world the sexual services are to be provided and whether those services are provided,

(b)   whether A is, or ought to be, aware that C has engaged in exploitative conduct.

(3)   C engages in exploitative conduct if—

(a)   C uses force, threats (whether or not relating to violence) or any other form of coercion, or

(b)   C practises any form of deception.

(4)   A person guilty of an offence under this section is liable on summary conviction to a fine not exceeding level 3 on the standard scale.]

PART 1
SEXUAL OFFENCES

TRAFFICKING

57   Trafficking into the UK for sexual exploitation

(1)   A person commits an offence if he intentionally arranges or facilitates the arrival in [, or the entry into,] the United Kingdom of another person (B) and either—

(a)   he intends to do anything to or in respect of B, after B's arrival but in any part of the world, which if done will involve the commission of a relevant offence, or

(b)   he believes that another person is likely to do something to or in respect of B, after B's arrival but in any part of the world, which if done will involve the commission of a relevant offence.

(2)   A person guilty of an offence under this section is liable—

(a)   on summary conviction, to imprisonment for a term not exceeding 6 months or a fine not exceeding the statutory maximum or both;

(b)   on conviction on indictment, to imprisonment for a term not exceeding 14 years.

58   Trafficking within the UK for sexual exploitation

(1)   A person commits an offence if he intentionally arranges or facilitates travel within the United Kingdom by another person (B) and either—

(a)   he intends to do anything to or in respect of B, during or after the journey and in any part of the world, which if done will involve the commission of a relevant offence, or

(b)   he believes that another person is likely to do something to or in respect of B, during or after the journey and in any part of the world, which if done will involve the commission of a relevant offence.

(2)   A person guilty of an offence under this section is liable—

(a)   on summary conviction, to imprisonment for a term not exceeding 6 months or a fine not exceeding the statutory maximum or both;

(b)   on conviction on indictment, to imprisonment for a term not exceeding 14 years.

59   **Trafficking out of the UK for sexual exploitation**

(1)   A person commits an offence if he intentionally arranges or facilitates the departure from the United Kingdom of another person (B) and either—

(a)   he intends to do anything to or in respect of B, after B's departure but in any part of the world, which if done will involve the commission of a relevant offence, or

(b)   he believes that another person is likely to do something to or in respect of B, after B's departure but in any part of the world, which if done will involve the commission of a relevant offence.

(2)   A person guilty of an offence under this section is liable—

(a)   on summary conviction, to imprisonment for a term not exceeding 6 months or a fine not exceeding the statutory maximum or both;

(b)   on conviction on indictment, to imprisonment for a term not exceeding 14 years.

[59A   Trafficking people for sexual exploitation

(1)   A person ("A") commits an offence if A intentionally arranges or facilitates—

(a)   the arrival in, or entry into, the United Kingdom or another country of another person ("B"),

(b)   the travel of B within the United Kingdom or another country, or

(c)   the departure of B from the United Kingdom or another country,

with a view to the sexual exploitation of B.

(2)   For the purposes of subsection (1)(a) and (c) A's arranging or facilitating is with a view to the sexual exploitation of B if, and only if—

(a)   A intends to do anything to or in respect of B, after B's arrival, entry or (as the case may be) departure but in any part of the world, which if done will involve the commission of a relevant offence, or

(b)   A believes that another person is likely to do something to or in respect of B, after B's arrival, entry or (as the case may be) departure but in any part of the world, which if done will involve the commission of a relevant offence.

(3)   For the purposes of subsection (1)(b) A's arranging or facilitating is with a view to the sexual exploitation of B if, and only if—

(a)   A intends to do anything to or in respect of B, during or after the journey and in any part of the world, which if done will involve the commission of a relevant offence, or

(b)   A believes that another person is likely to do something to or in respect of B, during or after the journey and in any part of the world, which if done will involve the commission of a relevant offence.

(4)   A person who is a UK national commits an offence under this section regardless of—

(a)   where the arranging or facilitating takes place, or

(b)   which country is the country of arrival, entry, travel or (as the case may be) departure.

(5)   A person who is not a UK national commits an offence under this section if —

(a)   any part of the arranging or facilitating takes place in the United Kingdom, or

(b)   the United Kingdom is the country of arrival, entry, travel or (as the case may be) departure.

(6)   A person guilty of an offence under this section is liable—

(a)   on summary conviction, to imprisonment for a term not exceeding 12 months or a fine not exceeding the statutory maximum or both;

(b)   on conviction on indictment, to imprisonment for a term not exceeding 14 years.

(7)   In relation to an offence committed before the commencement of section 154(1) of the Criminal Justice Act 2003, the reference in subsection (6)(a) to 12 months is to be read as a reference to 6 months.]

60   [Section 59A: interpretation]

(1)   [In section 59A—

"country" includes any territory or other part of the world;

"relevant offence" means—

(a)   any offence under the law of England and Wales which is an offence under this Part or under section 1(1)(a) of the Protection of Children Act 1978, or

(b)   anything done outside England and Wales which is not an offence within paragraph (a) but would be if done in England and Wales;

"UK national" means—

(a)   a British citizen,

(b)   a person who is a British subject by virtue of Part 4 of the British Nationality Act 1981 and who has the right of abode in the United Kingdom, or

(c)   a person who is a British overseas territories citizen by virtue of a connection with Gibraltar.]

[...]   [. . . . .]

[...]   [...]

[...]   [...]

[...]   [...]

[...]   [...]

[...]   [...]

[...]   [...]

[...]   [...]

[(2)   Sections 57 to 59 apply to anything done whether inside or outside the United Kingdom.]

[60A   **Forfeiture of land vehicle, ship or aircraft**

(1)   This section applies if a person is convicted on indictment of an offence under [section 59A.

(2)   The court may order the forfeiture of a land vehicle used or intended to be used in connection with the offence if the convicted person—

(a)   owned the vehicle at the time the offence was committed;

(b)   was at that time a director, secretary or manager of a company which owned the vehicle;

(c)   was at that time in possession of the vehicle under a hire-purchase agreement;

(d)   was at that time a director, secretary or manager of a company which was in possession of the vehicle under a hire-purchase agreement; or

(e)   was driving the vehicle in the course of the commission of the offence.

(3)   The court may order the forfeiture of a ship or aircraft used or intended to be used in connection with the offence if the convicted person—

(a)   owned the ship or aircraft at the time the offence was committed;

(b)   was at that time a director, secretary or manager of a company which owned the ship or aircraft;

(c)   was at that time in possession of the ship or aircraft under a hire-purchase agreement;

(d)   was at that time a director, secretary or manager of a company which was in possession of the ship or aircraft under a hire-purchase agreement;

(e)   was at that time a charterer of the ship or aircraft; or

(f)   committed the offence while acting as captain of the ship or aircraft.

(4)   But in a case to which subsection (3)(a) or (b) does not apply, forfeiture may be ordered only—

(a)   in the case of a ship, if subsection (5) or (6) applies;

(b)   in the case of an aircraft, if subsection (5) or (7) applies.

(5)   This subsection applies where a person who, at the time the offence was committed, owned the ship or aircraft or was a director, secretary or manager of a company which owned it, knew or ought to have known of the intention to use it in the course of the commission of an offence under section 59A].

(6)   This subsection applies where a ship's gross tonnage is less than 500 tons.

(7)   This subsection applies where the maximum weight at which an aircraft (which is not a hovercraft) may take off in accordance with its certificate of airworthiness is less than 5,700 kilogrammes.

(8)   Where a person who claims to have an interest in a land vehicle, ship or aircraft applies to a court to make representations on the question of forfeiture, the court may not make an order under this section in respect of the vehicle, ship or aircraft unless the person has been given an opportunity to make representations.

60B   Detention of land vehicle, ship or aircraft

(1)   If a person has been arrested for an offence under [section 59A], a constable or a senior immigration officer may detain a relevant vehicle, ship or aircraft —

    (a)   until a decision is taken as to whether or not to charge the arrested person with that offence;

    (b)   if the arrested person has been charged, until he is acquitted, the charge against him is dismissed or the proceedings are discontinued; or

    (c)   if he has been charged and convicted, until the court decides whether or not to order forfeiture of the vehicle, ship or aircraft.

(2)   A vehicle, ship or aircraft is a relevant vehicle, ship or aircraft, in relation to an arrested person if it is a land vehicle, ship or aircraft which the constable or officer concerned has reasonable grounds for believing could, on conviction of the arrested person for the offence for which he was arrested, be the subject of an order for forfeiture made under section 60A.

(3)   A person (other than the arrested person) may apply to the court for the release of a land vehicle, ship or aircraft on the grounds that—

    (a)   he owns the vehicle, ship or aircraft;

    (b)   he was, immediately before the detention of the vehicle, ship or aircraft, in possession of it under a hire-purchase agreement; or

    (c)   he is a charterer of the ship or aircraft.

(4)   The court to which an application is made under subsection (3) may, on such security or surety being tendered as it considers satisfactory, release the vehicle, ship or aircraft on condition that it is made available to the court if—

    (a)   the arrested person is convicted; and

      (b)   an order for its forfeiture is made under section 60A.

(5)   In this section, "court" means—

      (a)   in relation to England and Wales—

           (i)   if the arrested person has not been charged, or he has been charged but proceedings for the offence have not begun to be heard, a magistrates' court;

           (ii)   if he has been charged and proceedings for the offence are being heard, the court hearing the proceedings;

      (b)   in relation to Northern Ireland—

           (i)   if the arrested person has not been charged, a magistrates' court for the county court division in which he was arrested;

           (ii)   if he has been charged but proceedings for the offence have not begun to be heard, a magistrates' court for the county court division in which he was charged;

           (iii)   if he has been charged and proceedings for the offence are being heard, the court hearing the proceedings.

(6)   In this section, "senior immigration officer" means an immigration officer (appointed or employed as such under the Immigration Act 1971) not below the rank of chief immigration officer.

60C   Sections 60A and 60B: interpretation

(1)   In this section and sections 60A and 60B, unless the contrary intention appears—

"aircraft" includes hovercraft;

"captain" means master (of a ship) or commander (of an aircraft);

"land vehicle" means any vehicle other than a ship or aircraft;

"ship" includes every description of vessel used in navigation.

(2)   In sections 60A and 60B, a reference to being an owner of a vehicle, ship or aircraft includes a reference to being any of a number of persons who jointly own it.]

PREPARATORY OFFENCES

61   Administering a substance with intent

(1)   A person commits an offence if he intentionally administers a substance to, or causes a substance to be taken by, another person (B)—

      (a)   knowing that B does not consent, and

      (b)   with the intention of stupefying or overpowering B, so as to enable any person to engage in a sexual activity that involves B.

(2)   A person guilty of an offence under this section is liable—

(a)   on summary conviction, to imprisonment for a term not exceeding 6 months or a fine not exceeding the statutory maximum or both;

(b)   on conviction on indictment, to imprisonment for a term not exceeding 10 years.

62   Committing an offence with intent to commit a sexual offence

(1)   A person commits an offence under this section if he commits any offence with the intention of committing a relevant sexual offence.

(2)   In this section, "relevant sexual offence" means any offence under this Part (including an offence of aiding, abetting, counselling or procuring such an offence).

(3)   A person guilty of an offence under this section is liable on conviction on indictment, where the offence is committed by kidnapping or false imprisonment, to imprisonment for life.

(4)   Unless subsection (3) applies, a person guilty of an offence under this section is liable—

(a)   on summary conviction, to imprisonment for a term not exceeding 6 months or a fine not exceeding the statutory maximum or both;

(b)   on conviction on indictment, to imprisonment for a term not exceeding 10 years.

63   Trespass with intent to commit a sexual offence

(1)   A person commits an offence if—

(a)   he is a trespasser on any premises,

(b)   he intends to commit a relevant sexual offence on the premises, and

(c)   he knows that, or is reckless as to whether, he is a trespasser.

(2)   In this section—

"premises" includes a structure or part of a structure;

"relevant sexual offence" has the same meaning as in section 62;

"structure" includes a tent, vehicle or vessel or other temporary or movable structure.

(3)   A person guilty of an offence under this section is liable—

(a)   on summary conviction, to imprisonment for a term not exceeding 6 months or a fine not exceeding the statutory maximum or both;

(b)   on conviction on indictment, to imprisonment for a term not exceeding 10 years.

SEX WITH AN ADULT RELATIVE

64   Sex with an adult relative: penetration

(1)   A person aged 16 or over (A) [(subject to subsection (3A))] commits an offence if—

(a)   he intentionally penetrates another person's vagina or anus with a part of his body or anything else, or penetrates another person's mouth with his penis,

(b)   the penetration is sexual,

(c)   the other person (B) is aged 18 or over,

(d)   A is related to B in a way mentioned in subsection (2), and

(e)   A knows or could reasonably be expected to know that he is related to B in that way.

(2)   The ways that A may be related to B are as parent, grandparent, child, grandchild, brother, sister, half-brother, half-sister, uncle, aunt, nephew or niece.

(3)   In subsection (2)—

[(za)   "parent" includes an adoptive parent;

(zb)   "child" includes an adopted person within the meaning of Chapter 4 of Part 1 of the Adoption and Children Act 2002;]

(a)   "uncle" means the brother of a person's parent, and "aunt" has a corresponding meaning;

(b)   "nephew" means the child of a person's brother or sister, and "niece" has a corresponding meaning.

[(3A)   Where subsection (1) applies in a case where A is related to B as B's child by virtue of subsection (3)(zb), A does not commit an offence under this section unless A is 18 or over.]

(4)   Where in proceedings for an offence under this section it is proved that the defendant was related to the other person in any of those ways, it is to be taken that the defendant knew or could reasonably have been expected to know that he was related in that way unless sufficient evidence is adduced to raise an issue as to whether he knew or could reasonably have been expected to know that he was.

(5)   A person guilty of an offence under this section is liable—

(a)   on summary conviction, to imprisonment for a term not exceeding 6 months or a fine not exceeding the statutory maximum or both;

(b)   on conviction on indictment, to imprisonment for a term not exceeding 2 years.

[(6)   Nothing in—

(a)   section 47 of the Adoption Act 1976 (which disapplies the status provisions in section 39 of that Act for the purposes of this section in relation to adoptions before 30 December 2005), or

(b)   section 74 of the Adoption and Children Act 2002 (which disapplies the status provisions in section 67 of that Act for those purposes in relation to adoptions on or after that date),

is to be read as preventing the application of section 39 of the Adoption Act 1976 or section 67 of the Adoption and Children Act 2002 for the purposes of subsection (3)(za) and (zb) above.]

65   **Sex with an adult relative: consenting to penetration**

(1)   A person aged 16 or over (A) [(subject to subsection (3A))] commits an offence if—

   (a)   another person (B) penetrates A's vagina or anus with a part of B's body or anything else, or penetrates A's mouth with B's penis,

   (b)   A consents to the penetration,

   (c)   the penetration is sexual,

   (d)   B is aged 18 or over,

   (e)   A is related to B in a way mentioned in subsection (2), and

   (f)   A knows or could reasonably be expected to know that he is related to B in that way.

(2)   The ways that A may be related to B are as parent, grandparent, child, grandchild, brother, sister, half-brother, half-sister, uncle, aunt, nephew or niece.

(3)   In subsection (2)—

   [(za)   "parent" includes an adoptive parent;

   (zb)   "child" includes an adopted person within the meaning of Chapter 4 of Part 1 of the Adoption and Children Act 2002;]

   (a)   "uncle" means the brother of a person's parent, and "aunt" has a corresponding meaning;

   (b)   "nephew" means the child of a person's brother or sister, and "niece" has a corresponding meaning.

[(3A)   Where subsection (1) applies in a case where A is related to B as B's child by virtue of subsection (3)(zb), A does not commit an offence under this section unless A is 18 or over.]

(4)   Where in proceedings for an offence under this section it is proved that the defendant was related to the other person in any of those ways, it is to be taken that the defendant knew or could reasonably have been expected to know that he was related in that way unless sufficient evidence is adduced to raise an issue as to whether he knew or could reasonably have been expected to know that he was.

(5)   A person guilty of an offence under this section is liable—

   (a)   on summary conviction, to imprisonment for a term not exceeding 6 months or a fine not exceeding the statutory maximum or both;

   (b)   on conviction on indictment, to imprisonment for a term not exceeding 2 years.

[(6)   Nothing in—

   (a)   section 47 of the Adoption Act 1976 (which disapplies the status provisions in section 39 of that Act for the purposes of this section in relation to adoptions before 30 December 2005), or

(b)   section 74 of the Adoption and Children Act 2002 (which disapplies the status provisions in section 67 of that Act for those purposes in relation to adoptions on or after that date),

is to be read as preventing the application of section 39 of the Adoption Act 1976 or section 67 of the Adoption and Children Act 2002 for the purposes of subsection (3)(za) and (zb) above.]

OTHER OFFENCES

66   Exposure

(1)   A person commits an offence if—

(a)   he intentionally exposes his genitals, and

(b)   he intends that someone will see them and be caused alarm or distress.

(2)   A person guilty of an offence under this section is liable—

(a)   on summary conviction, to imprisonment for a term not exceeding 6 months or a fine not exceeding the statutory maximum or both;

(b)   on conviction on indictment, to imprisonment for a term not exceeding 2 years.

67   Voyeurism

(1)   A person commits an offence if—

(a)   for the purpose of obtaining sexual gratification, he observes another person doing a private act, and

(b)   he knows that the other person does not consent to being observed for his sexual gratification.

(2)   A person commits an offence if—

(a)   he operates equipment with the intention of enabling another person to observe, for the purpose of obtaining sexual gratification, a third person (B) doing a private act, and

(b)   he knows that B does not consent to his operating equipment with that intention.

(3)   A person commits an offence if—

(a)   he records another person (B) doing a private act,

(b)   he does so with the intention that he or a third person will, for the purpose of obtaining sexual gratification, look at an image of B doing the act, and

(c)   he knows that B does not consent to his recording the act with that intention.

(4)   A person commits an offence if he instals equipment, or constructs or adapts a structure or part of a structure, with the intention of enabling himself or another person to commit an offence under subsection (1).

(5)   A person guilty of an offence under this section is liable—

(a)   on summary conviction, to imprisonment for a term not exceeding 6 months or a fine not exceeding the statutory maximum or both;

(b)   on conviction on indictment, to imprisonment for a term not exceeding 2 years.

68   **Voyeurism: interpretation**

(1)   For the purposes of section 67, a person is doing a private act if the person is in a place which, in the circumstances, would reasonably be expected to provide privacy, and—

(a)   the person's genitals, buttocks or breasts are exposed or covered only with underwear,

(b)   the person is using a lavatory, or

(c)   the person is doing a sexual act that is not of a kind ordinarily done in public.

(2)   In section 67, "structure" includes a tent, vehicle or vessel or other temporary or movable structure.

69   **Intercourse with an animal**

(1)   A person commits an offence if—

(a)   he intentionally performs an act of penetration with his penis,

(b)   what is penetrated is the vagina or anus of a living animal, and

(c)   he knows that, or is reckless as to whether, that is what is penetrated.

(2)   A person (A) commits an offence if—

(a)   A intentionally causes, or allows, A's vagina or anus to be penetrated,

(b)   the penetration is by the penis of a living animal, and

(c)   A knows that, or is reckless as to whether, that is what A is being penetrated by.

(3)   A person guilty of an offence under this section is liable—

(a)   on summary conviction, to imprisonment for a term not exceeding 6 months or a fine not exceeding the statutory maximum or both;

(b)   on conviction on indictment, to imprisonment for a term not exceeding 2 years.

70   **Sexual penetration of a corpse**

(1)   A person commits an offence if—

(a)   he intentionally performs an act of penetration with a part of his body or anything else,

(b)   what is penetrated is a part of the body of a dead person,

(c)   he knows that, or is reckless as to whether, that is what is penetrated, and

(d)   the penetration is sexual.

(2)   A person guilty of an offence under this section is liable—

(a)   on summary conviction, to imprisonment for a term not exceeding 6 months or a fine not exceeding the statutory maximum or both;

(b)   on conviction on indictment, to imprisonment for a term not exceeding 2 years.

71   Sexual activity in a public lavatory

(1)   A person commits an offence if—

(a)   he is in a lavatory to which the public or a section of the public has or is permitted to have access, whether on payment or otherwise,

(b)   he intentionally engages in an activity, and,

(c)   the activity is sexual.

(2)   For the purposes of this section, an activity is sexual if a reasonable person would, in all the circumstances but regardless of any person's purpose, consider it to be sexual.

(3)   A person guilty of an offence under this section is liable on summary conviction, to imprisonment for a term not exceeding 6 months or a fine not exceeding level 5 on the standard scale or both.

OFFENCES OUTSIDE THE UNITED KINGDOM

[72   Offences outside the United Kingdom

(1)   If—

(a)   a United Kingdom national does an act in a country outside the United Kingdom, and

(b)   the act, if done in England and Wales or Northern Ireland, would constitute a sexual offence to which this section applies,

the United Kingdom national is guilty in that part of the United Kingdom of that sexual offence.

(2)   If—

(a)   a United Kingdom resident does an act in a country outside the United Kingdom,

(b)   the act constitutes an offence under the law in force in that country, and

(c)   the act, if done in England and Wales or Northern Ireland, would constitute a sexual offence to which this section applies,

the United Kingdom resident is guilty in that part of the United Kingdom of that sexual offence.

(3)   If—

      (a)   a person does an act in a country outside the United Kingdom at a time when the person was not a United Kingdom national or a United Kingdom resident,

      (b)   the act constituted an offence under the law in force in that country,

      (c)   the act, if done in England and Wales or Northern Ireland, would have constituted a sexual offence to which this section applies, and

      (d)   the person meets the residence or nationality condition at the relevant time,

proceedings may be brought against the person in that part of the United Kingdom for that sexual offence as if the person had done the act there.

(4)   The person meets the residence or nationality condition at the relevant time if the person is a United Kingdom national or a United Kingdom resident at the time when the proceedings are brought.

(5)   An act punishable under the law in force in any country constitutes an offence under that law for the purposes of subsections (2) and (3) however it is described in that law.

(6)   The condition in subsection (2)(b) or (3)(b) is to be taken to be met unless, not later than rules of court may provide, the defendant serves on the prosecution a notice—

      (a)   stating that, on the facts as alleged with respect to the act in question, the condition is not in the defendant's opinion met,

      (b)   showing the grounds for that opinion, and

      (c)   requiring the prosecution to prove that it is met.

(7)   But the court, if it thinks fit, may permit the defendant to require the prosecution to prove that the condition is met without service of a notice under subsection (6).

(8)   In the Crown Court the question whether the condition is met is to be decided by the judge alone.

(9)   In this section—

"country" includes territory;

"United Kingdom national" means an individual who is—

      (a)   a British citizen, a British overseas territories citizen, a British National (Overseas) or a British Overseas citizen;

      (b)   a person who under the British Nationality Act 1981 is a British subject; or

      (c)   a British protected person within the meaning of that Act;

"United Kingdom resident" means an individual who is resident in the United Kingdom.

(10)   Schedule 2 lists the sexual offences to which this section applies.]

SUPPLEMENTARY AND GENERAL

73   **Exceptions to aiding, abetting and counselling**

(1)   A person is not guilty of aiding, abetting or counselling the commission against a child of an offence to which this section applies if he acts for the purpose of—

(a)   protecting the child from sexually transmitted infection,

(b)   protecting the physical safety of the child,

(c)   preventing the child from becoming pregnant, or

(d)   promoting the child's emotional well-being by the giving of advice,

and not for the purpose of obtaining sexual gratification or for the purpose of causing or encouraging the activity constituting the offence or the child's participation in it.

(2)   This section applies to—

(a)   an offence under any of sections 5 to 7 (offences against children under 13);

(b)   an offence under section 9 (sexual activity with a child);

(c)   an offence under section 13 which would be an offence under section 9 if the offender were aged 18;

(d)   an offence under any of sections 16, 25, 30, 34 and 38 (sexual activity) against a person under 16.

(3)   This section does not affect any other enactment or any rule of law restricting the circumstances in which a person is guilty of aiding, abetting or counselling an offence under this Part.

74   **"Consent"**

For the purposes of this Part, a person consents if he agrees by choice, and has the freedom and capacity to make that choice.

75   **Evidential presumptions about consent**

(1)   If in proceedings for an offence to which this section applies it is proved—

(a)   that the defendant did the relevant act,

(b)   that any of the circumstances specified in subsection (2) existed, and

(c)   that the defendant knew that those circumstances existed,

the complainant is to be taken not to have consented to the relevant act unless sufficient evidence is adduced to raise an issue as to whether he consented, and the defendant is to be taken not to have reasonably believed that the complainant consented unless sufficient evidence is adduced to raise an issue as to whether he reasonably believed it.

(2)   The circumstances are that—

(a)   any person was, at the time of the relevant act or immediately before it began, using violence against the complainant or causing the complainant to fear that immediate violence would be used against him;

(b)   any person was, at the time of the relevant act or immediately before it began, causing the complainant to fear that violence was being used, or that immediate violence would be used, against another person;

(c)   the complainant was, and the defendant was not, unlawfully detained at the time of the relevant act;

(d)   the complainant was asleep or otherwise unconscious at the time of the relevant act;

(e)   because of the complainant's physical disability, the complainant would not have been able at the time of the relevant act to communicate to the defendant whether the complainant consented;

(f)   any person had administered to or caused to be taken by the complainant, without the complainant's consent, a substance which, having regard to when it was administered or taken, was capable of causing or enabling the complainant to be stupefied or overpowered at the time of the relevant act.

(3)   In subsection (2)(a) and (b), the reference to the time immediately before the relevant act began is, in the case of an act which is one of a continuous series of sexual activities, a reference to the time immediately before the first sexual activity began.

76 Conclusive presumptions about consent

(1)   If in proceedings for an offence to which this section applies it is proved that the defendant did the relevant act and that any of the circumstances specified in subsection (2) existed, it is to be conclusively presumed—

(a)   that the complainant did not consent to the relevant act, and

(b)   that the defendant did not believe that the complainant consented to the relevant act.

(2)   The circumstances are that—

(a)   the defendant intentionally deceived the complainant as to the nature or purpose of the relevant act;

(b)   the defendant intentionally induced the complainant to consent to the relevant act by impersonating a person known personally to the complainant.

77 Sections 75 and 76: relevant acts

In relation to an offence to which sections 75 and 76 apply, references in those sections to the relevant act and to the complainant are to be read as follows—

Offence	*Relevant Act*
An offence under section 1 (rape).	The defendant intentionally penetrating, with his penis, the vagina, anus or mouth of another person ("").
An offence under section 2 (assault by penetration).	The defendant intentionally penetrating, with a part of his body or anything else, the vagina or anus of another person (""), where the penetration is sexual.
An offence under section 3 (sexual assault).	The defendant intentionally touching another person (""), where the touching is sexual.
An offence under section 4 (causing a person to engage in sexual activity without consent).	The defendant intentionally causing another person ("") to engage in an activity, where the activity is sexual.

78   **"Sexual"**

For the purposes of this Part (except section 71), penetration, touching or any other activity is sexual if a reasonable person would consider that—

(a)   whatever its circumstances or any person's purpose in relation to it, it is because of its nature sexual, or

(b)   because of its nature it may be sexual and because of its circumstances or the purpose of any person in relation to it (or both) it is sexual.

79   **Part 1: general interpretation**

(1)   The following apply for the purposes of this Part.

(2)   Penetration is a continuing act from entry to withdrawal.

(3)   References to a part of the body include references to a part surgically constructed (in particular, through gender reassignment surgery).

(4)   "Image" means a moving or still image and includes an image produced by any means and, where the context permits, a three-dimensional image.

(5)   References to an image of a person include references to an image of an imaginary person.

(6)   "Mental disorder" has the meaning given by section 1 of the Mental Health Act 1983 (c. 20).

(7)   References to observation (however expressed) are to observation whether direct or by looking at an image.

(8)   Touching includes touching—

(a)   with any part of the body,

(b)   with anything else,

(c)   through anything,

and in particular includes touching amounting to penetration.

(9)   "Vagina" includes vulva.

(10)   In relation to an animal, references to the vagina or anus include references to any similar part.

PART 2
NOTIFICATION AND ORDERS

NOTIFICATION ORDERS

98   Notification orders: effect

(1)   Where a notification order is made—

    (a)   the application of this Part to the defendant in respect of the conviction, finding or caution to which the order relates is subject to the modifications set out below, and

    (b)   subject to those modifications, the defendant becomes or (as the case may be) remains subject to the notification requirements of this Part for the notification period set out in section 82.

(2)   The "relevant date" means—

    (a)   in the case of a person within section 97(2)(a), the date of the conviction;

    (b)   in the case of a person within section 97(2)(b) or (c), the date of the finding;

    (c)   in the case of a person within section 97(2)(d), the date of the caution.

(3)   In section 82—

    (a)   references, except in the Table, to a person (or relevant offender) within any provision of section 80 are to be read as references to the defendant;

    (b)   the reference in the Table to section 80(1)(d) is to be read as a reference to section 97(2)(d);

    (c)   references to an order of any description are to be read as references to any corresponding disposal made in relation to the defendant in respect of an offence or finding by reference to which the notification order was made;

    (d)   the reference to offences listed in Schedule 3 is to be read as a reference to relevant offences.

(4)   In sections 83 and 85, references to the commencement of this Part are to be read as references to the date of service of the notification order.

Theft Act 1968

1968 c. 60

DEFINITION OF "THEFT"

1   **Basic definition of theft**

(1)   A person is guilty of theft if he dishonestly appropriates property belonging to another with the intention of permanently depriving the other of it; and " thief " and " steal " shall be construed accordingly.

(2)   It is immaterial whether the appropriation is made with a view to gain, or is made for the thief's own benefit.

(3)   The five following sections of this Act shall have effect as regards the interpretation and operation of this section (and, except as otherwise provided by this Act, shall apply only for purposes of this section).

2   **"Dishonestly"**

(1)   A person's appropriation of property belonging to another is not to be regarded as dishonest—

(a)   if he appropriates the property in the belief that he has in law the right to deprive the other of it, on behalf of himself or of a third person; or

(b)   if he appropriates the property in the belief that he would have the other's consent if the other knew of the appropriation and the circumstances of it; or

(c)   (except where the property came to him as trustee or personal representative) if he appropriates the property in the belief that the person to whom the property belongs cannot be discovered by taking reasonable steps.

(2)   A person's appropriation of property belonging to another may be dishonest notwithstanding that he is willing to pay for the property.

3   **"Appropriates"**

(1)   Any assumption by a person of the rights of an owner amounts to an appropriation, and this includes, where he has come by the property (innocently or not) without stealing it, any later assumption of a right to it by keeping or dealing with it as owner.

(2)   Where property or a right or interest in property is or purports to be transferred for value to a person acting in good faith, no later assumption by him of rights which he believed himself to be acquiring shall, by reason of any defect in the transferor's title, amount to theft of the property.

4   "Property"

    (1)   " Property " includes money and all other property, real or personal, including things in action and other intangible property.

    (2)   A person cannot steal land, or things forming part of land and severed from it by him or by his directions, except in the following cases, that it to say—

        (a)   when he is a trustee or personal representative, or is authorised by power of attorney, or as liquidator of a company, or otherwise, to sell or dispose of land belonging to another, and he appropriates the land or anything forming part of it by dealing with it in breach of the confidence reposed in him; or

        (b)   when he is not in possession of the land and appropriates anything forming part of the land by severing it or causing it to be severed, or after it has been severed; or

        (c)   when, being in possession of the land under a tenancy, he appropriates the whole or part of any fixture or structure let to be used with the land.

    For purposes of this subsection " land " does not include incorporeal hereditaments; " tenancy " means a tenancy for years or any less period and includes an agreement for such a tenancy, but a person who after the end of a tenancy remains in possession as staututory tenant or otherwise is to be treated as having possession under the tenancy, and " let " shall be construed accordingly.

    (3)   A person who picks mushrooms growing wild on any land, or who picks flowers, fruit or foliage from a plant growing wild on any land, does not (although not in possession of the land) steal what he picks, unless he does it for reward or for sale or other commercial purpose.

    For purposes of this subsection " mushroom " includes any fungus, and " plant " includes any shrub or tree.

    (4)   Wild creatures, tamed or untamed, shall be regarded as property; but a person cannot steal a wild creature not tamed nor ordinarily kept in captivity, or the carcase of any such creature, unless either it has been reduced into possession by or on behalf of another person and possession of it has not since been lost or abandoned, or another person is in course of reducing it into possession.

5   "Belonging to another"

    (1)   Property shall be regarded as belonging to any person having possession or control of it, or having in it any proprietary right or interest (not being an equitable interest arising only from an agreement to transfer or grant an interest).

    (2)   Where property is subject to a trust, the persons to whom it belongs shall be regarded as including any person having a right to enforce the trust, and an intention to defeat the trust shall be regarded accordingly as an intention to

deprive of the property any person having that right.

(3)   Where a person receives property from or on account of another, and is under an obligation to the other to retain and deal with that property or its proceeds in a particular way, the property or proceeds shall be regarded (as against him) as belonging to the other.

(4)   Where a person gets property by another's mistake, and is under an obligation to make restoration (in whole or in part) of the property or its proceeds or of the value thereof, then to the extent of that obligation the property or proceeds shall be regarded (as against him) as belonging to the person entitled to restoration, and an intention not to make restoration shall be regarded accordingly as an intention to deprive that person of the property or proceeds.

(5)   Property of a corporation sole shall be regarded as belonging to the corporation notwithstanding a vacancy in the corporation.

6   "With the intention of permanently depriving the other of it"

(1)   A person appropriating property belonging to another without meaning the other permanently to lose the thing itself is nevertheless to be regarded as having the intention of permanently depriving the other of it if his intention is to treat the thing as his own to dispose of regardless of the other's rights; and a borrowing or lending of it may amount to so treating it if, but only if, the borrowing or lending is for a period and in circumstances making it equivalent to an outright taking or disposal.

(2)   Without prejudice to the generality of subsection (1) above, where a person, having possession or control (lawfully or not) of property belonging to another, parts with the property under a condition as to its return which he may not be able to perform, this (if done for purposes of his own and without the other's authority) amounts to treating the property as his own to dispose of regardless of the other's rights.

THEFT, ROBBERY, BURGLARY, ETC

7   Theft

A person guilty of theft shall on conviction on indictment be liable to imprisonment for a term not exceeding [seven years] .

8   Robbery

(1)   A person is guilty of robbery if he steals, and immediately before or at the time of doing so, and in order to do so, he uses force on any person or puts or seeks to put any person in fear of being then and there subjected to force.

(2)   A person guilty of robbery, or of an assault with intent to rob, shall on conviction on indictment be liable to imprisonment for life.

9   Burglary

(1)   A person is guilty of burglary if—

    (a)   he enters any building or part of a building as a trespasser and with intent to commit any such offence as is mentioned in subsection (2) below; or

    (b)   having entered any building or part of a building as a trespasser he steals or attempts to steal anything in the building or that part of it or inflicts or attempts to inflict on any person therein any grievous bodily harm.

(2)   The offences referred to in subsection (1)(a) above are offences of stealing anything in the building or part of a building in question, of inflicting on any person therein any grievous bodily harm . . . therein, and of doing unlawful damage to the building or anything therein.

[(3)   A person guilty of burglary shall on conviction on indictment be liable to imprisonment for a term not exceeding—

    (a)   where the offence was committed in respect of a building or part of a building which is a dwelling, fourteen years;

    (b)   in any other case, ten years.

(4)   References in subsections (1) and (2) above to a building, and the reference in subsection (3) above to a building which is a dwelling, shall apply also to an inhabited vehicle or vessel, and shall apply to any such vehicle or vessel at times when the person having a habitation in it is not there as well as at times when he is.]

10   Aggravated burglary

(1)   A person is guilty of aggravated burglary if he commits any burglary and at the time has with him any firearm or imitation firearm, any weapon of offence, or any explosive; and for this purpose—

    (a)   " firearm " includes an airgun or air pistol, and " imitation firearm " means anything which has the appearance of being a firearm, whether capable of being discharged or not; and

    (b)   " weapon of offence " means any article made or adapted for use for causing injury to or incapacitating a person, or intended by the person having it with him for such use; and

    (c)   " explosive " means any article manufactured for the purpose of producing a practical effect by explosion, or intended by the person having it with him for that purpose.

(2)   A person guilty of aggravated burglary shall on conviction on indictment be liable to imprisonment for life.

11   Removal of articles from places open to the public

(1)   Subject to subsections (2) and (3) below, where the public have access to a building in order to view the building or part of it, or a collection or part of

a collection housed in it, any person who without lawful authority removes from the building or its grounds the whole or part of any article displayed or kept for display to the public in the building or that part of it or in its grounds shall be guilty of an offence.

For this purpose " collection " includes a collection got together for a temporary purpose, but references in this section to a collection do not apply to a collection made or exhibited for the purpose of effecting sales or other commercial dealings.

(2)   It is immaterial for purposes of subsection (1) above, that the public's access to a building is limited to a particular period or particular occasion; but where anything removed from a building or its grounds is there otherwise than as forming part of, or being on loan for exhibition with, a collection intended for permanent exhibition to the public, the person removing it does not thereby commit an offence under this section unless he removes it on a day when the public have access to the building as mentioned in subsection (1) above.

(3)   A person does not commit an offence under this section if he believes that he has lawful authority for the removal of the thing in question or that he would have it if the person entitled to give it knew of the removal and the circum-stances of it.

(4)   A person guilty of an offence under this section shall, on conviction on indictment, be liable to imprisonment for a term not exceeding five years.

12   **Taking motor vehicle or other conveyance without authority**

(1)   Subject to subsections (5) and (6) below, a person shall be guilty of an offence if, without having the consent of the owner or other lawful authority, he takes any conveyance for his own or another's use or, knowing that any conveyance has been taken without such authority, drives it or allows himself to be carried in or on it.

(2)   A person guilty of an offence under subsection (1) above shall [be liable on summary conviction to a fine not exceeding level 5 on the standard scale, to imprisonment for a term not exceeding six months, or to both.]

(3)   . . . .

(4)   If on the trial of an indictment for theft the jury are not satisfied that the accused committed theft, but it is proved that the accused committed an offence under subsection (1) above, the jury may find him guilty of the offence under subsection (1) [and if he is found guilty of it, he shall be liable as he would have been liable under subsection (2) above on summary conviction.]

[(4A)   Proceedings for an offence under subsection (1) above (but not proceedings of a kind falling within subsection (4) above) in relation to a mechanically propelled vehicle—

(a)   shall not be commenced after the end of the period of three years beginning with the day on which the offence was committed; but

(b)   subject to that, may be commenced at any time within the period of six months beginning with the relevant day.

(4B)   In subsection (4A)(b) above " the relevant day " means—

(a)   in the case of a prosecution for an offence under subsection (1) above by a public prosecutor, the day on which sufficient evidence to justify the proceedings came to the knowledge of any person responsible for deciding whether to commence any such prosecution;

(b)   in the case of a prosecution for an offence under subsection (1) above which is commenced by a person other than a public prosecutor after the discontinuance of a prosecution falling within paragraph (a) above which relates to the same facts, the day on which sufficient evidence to justify the proceedings came to the knowledge of the person who has decided to commence the prosecution or (if later) the discontinuance of the other prosecution;

(c)   in the case of any other prosecution for an offence under subsection (1) above, the day on which sufficient evidence to justify the proceedings came to the knowledge of the person who has decided to commence the prosecution.

(4C)   For the purposes of subsection (4A)(b) above a certificate of a person responsible for deciding whether to commence a prosecution of a kind mentioned in subsection (4B)(a) above as to the date on which such evidence as is mentioned in the certificate came to the knowledge of any person responsible for deciding whether to commence any such prosecution shall be conclusive evidence of that fact.]

(5)   Subsection (1) above shall not apply in relation to pedal cycles; but, subject to subsection (6) below, a person who, without having the consent of the owner or other lawful authority, takes a pedal cycle for his own or another's use, or rides a pedal cycle knowing it to have been taken without such authority, shall on summary conviction be liable to a fine not exceeding [level 3 on the standard scale.]

(6)   A person does not commit an offence under this section by anything done in the belief that he has lawful authority to do it or that he would have the owner's consent if the owner knew of his doing it and the circumstances of it.

(7)   For purposes of this section—

(a)   " conveyance " means any conveyance constructed or adapted for the carriage of a person or persons whether by land, water or air, except that it does not include a conveyance constructed or adapted for use only under the control of a person not carried in or on it, and " drive " shall be construed accordingly; and

(b)   " owner ", in relation to a conveyance which is the subject of a hiring agreement or hire-purchase agreement, means the person in possession of the conveyance under that agreement.

[12A   **Aggravated vehicle-taking**

(1)   Subject to subsection (3) below, a person is guilty of aggravated taking of a vehicle if—

(a)   he commits an offence under section 12(1) above (in this section referred to as a " basic offence ") in relation to a mechanically propelled vehicle; and

(b)   it is proved that, at any time after the vehicle was unlawfully taken (whether by him or another) and before it was recovered, the vehicle was driven, or injury or damage was caused, in one or more of the circumstances set out in paragraphs (a) to (d) of subsection (2) below.

(2)   The circumstances referred to in subsection (1)(b) above are—

(a)   that the vehicle was driven dangerously on a road or other public place;

(b)   that, owing to the driving of the vehicle, an accident occurred by which injury was caused to any person;

(c)   that, owing to the driving of the vehicle, an accident occurred by which damage was caused to any property, other than the vehicle;

(d)   that damage was caused to the vehicle.

(3)   A person is not guilty of an offence under this section if he proves that, as regards any such proven driving, injury or damage as is referred to in subsection (1)(b) above, either—

(a)   the driving, accident or damage referred to in subsection (2) above occurred before he committed the basic offence; or

(b)   he was neither in nor on nor in the immediate vicinity of the vehicle when that driving, accident or damage occurred.

(4)   A person guilty of an offence under this section shall be liable on conviction on indictment to imprisonment for a term not exceeding two years or, if it is proved that, in circumstances falling within subsection (2)(b) above, the accident caused the death of the person concerned, [fourteen years] .

(5)   If a person who is charged with an offence under this section is found not guilty of that offence but it is proved that he committed a basic offence, he may be convicted of the basic offence.

(6)   If by virtue of subsection (5) above a person is convicted of a basic offence before the Crown Court, that court shall have the same powers and duties as a magistrates' court would have had on convicting him of such an offence.

(7)   For the purposes of this section a vehicle is driven dangerously if—

(a)   it is driven in a way which falls far below what would be expected of a competent and careful driver; and

(b)   it would be obvious to a competent and careful driver that driving the vehicle in that way would be dangerous.

(8)   For the purposes of this section a vehicle is recovered when it is restored to its owner or to other lawful possession or custody; and in this subsection " owner " has the same meaning as in section 12 above.]

13   Abstracting of electricity

A person who dishonestly uses without due authority, or dishonestly causes to be wasted or diverted, any electricity shall on conviction on indictment be liable to imprisonment for a term not exceeding five years.

FRAUD AND BLACKMAIL

15   Obtaining property by deception

15A   Obtaining a money transfer by deception

15B   Section 15A: supplementary

16   Obtaining pecuniary advantage by deception

17   False accounting

(1)   Where a person dishonestly, with a view to gain for himself or another or with intent to cause loss to another,—

(a)   destroys, defaces, conceals or falsifies any account or any record or document made or required for any accounting purpose; or

(b)   in furnishing information for any purpose produces or makes use of any account, or any such record or document as aforesaid, which to his knowledge is or may be misleading, false or deceptive in a material particular;

he shall, on conviction on indictment, be liable to imprisonment for a term not exceeding seven years.

(2)   For purposes of this section a person who makes or concurs in making in an account or other document an entry which is or may be misleading, false or deceptive in a material particular, or who omits or concurs in omitting a material particular from an account or other document, is to be treated as falsifying the account or document.

18   Liability of company officers for certain offences by company

(1)   Where an offence committed by a body corporate under section . . . 17 of this Act is proved to have been committed with the consent or connivance of any director, manager, secretary or other similar officer of the body corporate, or any person who was purporting to act in any such capacity, he as well as the body corporate shall be guilty of that offence, and shall be liable to be proceeded against and punished accordingly.

(2)   Where the affairs of a body corporate are managed by its members, this section shall apply in relation to the acts and defaults of a member in connection with his functions of management as if he were a director of the body corporate.

19   **False statements by company directors, etc**

(1)   Where an officer of a body corporate or unincorporated association (or person purporting to act as such), with intent to deceive members or creditors of the body corporate or association about its affairs, publishes or concurs in publishing a written statement or account which to his knowledge is or may be misleading, false or deceptive in a material particular, he shall on conviction on indictment be liable to imprisonment for a term not exceeding seven years.

(2)   For purposes of this section a person who has entered into a security for the benefit of a body corporate or association is to be treated as a creditor of it.

(3)   Where the affairs of a body corporate or association are managed by its members, this section shall apply to any statement which a member publishes or concurs in publishing in connection with his functions of management as if he were an officer of the body corporate or association.

20   **Suppression, etc. of documents**

(1)   A person who dishonestly, with a view to gain for himself or another or with intent to cause loss to another, destroys, defaces or conceals any valuable security, any will or other testamentary document or any original document of or belonging to, or filed or deposited in, any court of justice or any government department shall on conviction on indictment be liable to imprisonment for a term not exceeding seven years.

(2)   . . . .

21   **Blackmail**

(1)   A person is guilty of blackmail if, with a view to gain for himself or another or with intent to cause loss to another, he makes any unwarranted demand with menaces; and for this purpose a demand with menaces is unwarranted unless the person making it does so in the belief—

(a)   that he has reasonable grounds for making the demand; and

(b)   that the use of the menaces is a proper means of reinforcing the demand.

(2)   The nature of the act or omission demanded is immaterial, and it is also immaterial whether the menaces relate to action to be taken by the person making the demand.

(3)   A person guilty of blackmail shall on conviction on indictment be liable to imprisonment for a term not exceeding fourteen years.

OFFENCES RELATING TO GOODS STOLEN ETC

22 Handling stolen goods

(1) A person handles stolen goods if (otherwise than in the course of the stealing) knowing or believing them to be stolen goods he dishonestly receives the goods, or dishonestly undertakes or assists in their retention, removal, disposal or realisation by or for the benefit of another person, or if he arranges to do so.

(2) A person guilty of handling stolen goods shall on conviction on indictment be liable to imprisonment for a term not exceeding fourteen years.

23 Advertising rewards for return of goods stolen or lost

Where any public advertisement of a reward for the return of any goods which have been stolen or lost uses any words to the effect that no questions will be asked, or that the person producing the goods will be safe from apprehension or inquiry, or that any money paid for the purchase of the goods or advanced by way of loan on them will be repaid, the person advertising the reward and any person who prints or publishes the advertisement shall on summary conviction be liable to a fine not exceeding [level 3 on the standard scale.]

24 Scope of offences relating to stolen goods

(1) The provisions of this Act relating to goods which have been stolen shall apply whether the stealing occurred in England or Wales or elsewhere, and whether it occurred before or after the commencement of this Act, provided that the stealing (if not an offence under this Act) amounted to an offence where and at the time when the goods were stolen; and references to stolen goods shall be construed accordingly.

(2) For purposes of those provisions references to stolen goods shall include, in addition to the goods originally stolen and parts of them (whether in their original state or not),—

(a) any other goods which directly or indirectly represent or have at any time represented the stolen goods in the hands of the thief as being the proceeds of any disposal or realisation of the whole or part of the goods stolen or of goods so representing the stolen goods; and

(b) any other goods which directly or indirectly represent or have at any time represented the stolen goods in the hands of a handler of the stolen goods or any part of them as being the proceeds of any disposal or realisation of the whole or part of the stolen goods handled by him or of goods so representing them.

(3) But no goods shall be regarded as having continued to be stolen goods after they have been restored to the person from whom they were stolen or to other lawful possession or custody, or after that person and any other person claiming through him have otherwise ceased as regards those goods to have any right to restitution in respect of the theft.

(4)   For purposes of the provisions of this Act relating to goods which have been stolen (including subsections (1) to (3) above) goods obtained in England or Wales or elsewhere either by blackmail or [, subject to subsection (5) below, by fraud (within the meaning of the Fraud Act 2006)] shall be regarded as stolen; and " steal ", " theft " and " thief " shall be construed accordingly.

[(5)   Subsection (1) above applies in relation to goods obtained by fraud as if—

(a)   the reference to the commencement of this Act were a reference to the commencement of the Fraud Act 2006, and

(b)   the reference to an offence under this Act were a reference to an offence under section 1 of that Act.]

[24A   **Dishonestly retaining a wrongful credit**

(1)   A person is guilty of an offence if—

(a)   a wrongful credit has been made to an account kept by him or in respect of which he has any right or interest;

(b)   he knows or believes that the credit is wrongful; and

(c)   he dishonestly fails to take such steps as are reasonable in the circumstances to secure that the credit is cancelled.

(2)   References to a credit are to a credit of an amount of money.

[(2A)   A credit to an account is wrongful to the extent that it derives from—

(a)   theft;

(b)   blackmail;

(c)   fraud (contrary to section 1 of the Fraud Act 2006); or

(d)   stolen goods.]

(3)   . . . .

(4)   . . . .

(5)   In determining whether a credit to an account is wrongful, it is immaterial (in particular) whether the account is overdrawn before or after the credit is made.

(6)   A person guilty of an offence under this section shall be liable on conviction on indictment to imprisonment for a term not exceeding ten years.

(7)   Subsection (8) below applies for purposes of [provisions of this Act relating to stolen goods (including [subsection (2A)] above).

(8)   References to stolen goods include money which is dishonestly withdrawn from an account to which a wrongful credit has been made, but only to the extent that the money derives from the credit.

[(9)   " Account " means an account kept with—

(a)   a bank;

(b)   a person carrying on a business which falls within subsection (10) below; or

(c)   an issuer of electronic money (as defined for the purposes of Part 2 of the Financial Services and Markets Act 2000).

(10)   A business falls within this subsection if—

(a)   in the course of the business money received by way of deposit is lent to others; or

(b)   any other activity of the business is financed, wholly or to any material extent, out of the capital of or the interest on money received by way of deposit.

(11)   References in subsection (10) above to a deposit must be read with—

(a)   section 22 of the Financial Services and Markets Act 2000;

(b)   any relevant order under that section; and

(c)   Schedule 2 to that Act;

but any restriction on the meaning of deposit which arises from the identity of the person making it is to be disregarded.

(12)   For the purposes of subsection (10) above—

(a)   all the activities which a person carries on by way of business shall be regarded as a single business carried on by him; and

(b)   " money " includes money expressed in a currency other than sterling.]]

POSSESSION OF HOUSEBREAKING IMPLEMENTS, ETC

25   Going equipped for stealing, etc

(1)   A person shall be guilty of an offence if, when not at his place of abode, he has with him any article for use in the course of or in connection with any [burglary or theft] .

(2)   A person guilty of an offence under this section shall on conviction on indictment be liable to imprisonment for a term not exceeding three years.

(3)   Where a person is charged with an offence under this section, proof that he had with him any article made or adapted for use in committing a [burglary or theft] shall be evidence that he had it with him for such use.

(4)   . . . .

(5)   For purposes of this section an offence under section 12(1) of this Act of taking a conveyance shall be treated as theft . . . .

ENFORCEMENT AND PROCEDURE

27   Evidence and procedure on charge of theft or handling stolen goods

(1)   Any number of persons may be charged in one indictment, with reference to the same theft, with having at different times or at the same time handled all

or any of the stolen goods, and the persons so charged may be tried together.

(2) On the trial of two or more persons indicted for jointly handling any stolen goods the jury may find any of the accused guilty if the jury are satisfied that he handled all or any of the stolen goods, whether or not he did so jointly with the other accused or any of them.

(3) Where a person is being proceeded against for handling stolen goods (but not for any offence other than handling stolen goods), then at any stage of the proceedings, if evidence has been given of his having or arranging to have in his possession the goods the subject of the charge, or of his under-taking or assisting in, or arranging to undertake or assist in, their retention, removal, disposal or realisation, the following evidence shall be admissible for the purpose of proving that he knew or believed the goods to be stolen goods:—

(a) evidence that he has had in his possesion, or has undertaken or assisted in the retention, removal, disposal or realisation of, stolen goods from any theft taking place not earlier than twelve months before the offence charged; and

(b) (provided that seven days' notice in writing has been given to him of the intention to prove the conviction) evidence that he has within the five years preceding the date of the offence charged been convicted of theft or of handling stolen goods.

(4) In any proceedings for the theft of anything in the course of transmission (whether by post or otherwise), or for handling stolen goods from such a theft, a statutory declaration made by any person that he despatched or received or failed to receive any goods or postal packet, or that any goods or postal packet when despatched or received by him were in a particular state or condition, shall be admissible as evidence of the facts stated in the decla-ration, subject to the following conditions:—

(a) a statutory declaration shall only be admissible where and to the extent to which oral evidence to the like effect would have been admissible in the proceedings; and

(b) a statutory declaration shall only be admissible if at least seven days before the hearing or trial a copy of it has been given to the person charged, and he has not, at least three days before the hearing or trial or within such further time as the court may in special circum-stances allow, given the prosecutor written notice requiring the attendance at the hearing or trial of the person making the decla-ration.

[(4A) Where the proceedings mentioned in subsection (4) above are proceedings before a magistrates' court inquiring into an offence as examining justices that subsection shall have effect with the omission of the words from "subject to the following conditions" to the end of the subsection.]

(5) This section is to be construed in accordance with section 24 of this Act; and in subsection (3)(b) above the reference to handling stolen goods shall

include any corresponding offence committed before the commencement of this Act.

28   . . . .

GENERAL AND CONSEQUENTIAL PROVISIONS

30   [Spouses and civil partners]

(1)   This Act shall apply in relation to the parties to a marriage, and to property belonging to the wife or husband whether or not by reason of an interest derived from the marriage, as it would apply if they were not married and any such interest subsisted independently of the marriage.

(2)   Subject to subsection (4) below, a person shall have the same right to bring proceedings against that person's wife or husband for any offence (whether under this Act or otherwise) as if they were not married, and a person bringing any such proceedings shall be competent to give evidence for the prosecution at every stage of the proceedings.

(3)   . . . .

(4)   Proceedings shall not be instituted against a person for any offence of stealing or doing unlawful damage to property which at the time of the offence belongs to that person's wife or husband, [or civil partner] or for any attempt, incitement or conspiracy to commit such an offence, unless the proceedings are instituted by or with the consent of the Director of Public Prosecutions:

Provided that—

(a)   this subsection shall not apply to proceedings against a person for an offence—

      (i)   if that person is charged with committing the offence jointly with the wife or husband [or civil partner] ; . . .

      (ii)   if by virtue of any judicial decree or order (wherever made) that person and the wife or husband are at the time of the offence under no obligation to cohabit; . . .

      [or

      (iii)   an order (wherever made) is in force providing for the separation of that person and his or her civil partner.]

(b)   . . . .

(5)   Notwithstanding [section 6 of the Prosecution of Offences Act 1979] subsection (4) of this section shall apply—

(a)   to an arrest (if without warrant) made by the wife or husband, [or civil partner] and

(b)   to a warrant of arrest issued on an information laid by the wife or husband [or civil partner] .

32   **Effect on existing law and construction of references to offences**

(1)   The following offences are hereby abolished for all purposes not relating to offences committed before the commencement of this Act, that is to say—

(a)   any offence at common law of larceny, robbery, burglary, receiving stolen property, obtaining property by threats, extortion by colour or office or franchise, false accounting by public officers, concealment of treasure trove and, except as regards offences relating to the public revenue, cheating; and

(b)   any offence under an enactment mentioned in Part I of Schedule 3 to this Act, to the extent to which the offence depends on any section or part of a section included in column 3 of that Schedule;

but so that the provisions in Schedule 1 to this Act (which preserve with modifications certain offences under the Larcency Act 1861 of taking or killing deer and taking or destroying fish) shall have effect as there set out.

(2)   Except as regards offences committed before the commencement of this Act, and except in so far as the context otherwise requires,—

(a)   references in any enactment passed before this Act to an offence abolished by this Act shall, subject to any express amendment or repeal made by this Act, have effect as references to the corresponding offence under this Act, and in any such enactment the expression "receive"(when it relates to an offence of receiving) shall mean handle, and " receiver " shall be construed accordingly; and

(b)   without prejudice to paragraph (a) above, references in any enactment, whenever passed, to theft or stealing (including references to stolen goods), and references to robbery, blackmail, burglary, aggravated burglary or handling stolen goods, shall be construed in accordance with the provisions of this Act, including those of section 24.

SUPPLEMENTARY

34   **Interpretation**

(1)   Sections 4(1) and 5(1) of this Act shall apply generally for purposes of this Act as they apply for purposes of section 1.

(2)   For purposes of this Act—

(a)   " gain " and " loss " are to be construed as extending only to gain or loss in money or other property, but as extending to any such gain or loss whether temporary or permanent; and—

(i)   " gain " includes a gain by keeping what one has, as well as a gain by getting what one has not; and

(ii)   " loss " includes a loss by not getting what one might get, as well as a loss by parting with what one has;

(b) " goods ", except in so far as the context otherwise requires, includes money and every other description of property except land, and includes things severed from the land by stealing [; and.

(c) "mail bag" and "postal packet" have the meanings given by section 125(1) of the Postal Services Act 2000.]

Theft Act 1978

1978 c. 31

1 . . . .

2 . . . .

3 **Making off without payment.**

(1) Subject to subsection (3) below, a person who, knowing that payment on the spot for any goods supplied or service done is required or expected from him, dishonestly makes off without having paid as required or expected and with intent to avoid payment of the amount due shall be guilty of an offence.

(2) For purposes of this section "payment on the spot" includes payment at the time of collecting goods on which work has been done or in respect of which service has been provided.

(3) Subsection (1) above shall not apply where the supply of the goods or the doing of the service is contrary to law, or where the service done is such that payment is not legally enforceable.

(4) . . . .

5 **Supplementary.**

(1) . . . .

(2) Sections 30(1) (husband and wife), 31(1) (effect on civil proceedings) and 34 (interpretation) of the Theft Act 1968, so far as they are applicable in relation to this Act, shall apply as they apply in relation to that Act.

(3) . . . .

(4) In the Visiting Forces Act 1952, in paragraph 3 of the Schedule (which defines for England and Wales "offence against property" for purposes of the exclusion in certain cases of the jurisdiction of United Kingdom courts) there shall be added at the end—

"(j) the Theft Act 1978"

(5) In the Theft Act 1968 section 16(2)(a) is hereby repealed.

Index